JOBS & CAREERS

FREELANCE TEACHING & TUTORING

How to earn good money by teaching others what you know

Ison

WHAT'S THE SECRET OF BEING A GOOD TEACHER?

SELF PRESERVATION

How To Books

Cartoons by Mike Flanagan

British Library Cataloguing in Publication Data
A catalogue record for this book is available from the British Library.

Published by How To Books Ltd, 3 Newtec Place,
Magdalen Road, Oxford, OX4 1RE, United Kingdom.
Tel: (01865) 793806. Fax: (01865) 248780.

Note: The material contained in this book is set out in good faith for general
guidance and no liability can be accepted for loss or expense incurred as a result of
relying in particular circumstances on statements made in the book. The laws and
regulations are complex and liable to change, and readers should check the current
position with the relevant authorities before making personal arrangements.

Produced for How To Books by Deer Park Productions.
Typeset by Anneset, Weston super Mare, North Somerset
Printed and bound by Cromwell Press, Broughton Gifford, Melksham, Wiltshire

Contents

List of Illustrations

Preface

It is over ten years since I was an adult education principal and things have changed very dramatically since then. Public support for adult education has diminished, budgets have been cut throughout education, and local government services have been dismantled and emasculated by financial constraints and by the processes of privatisation and the devolution of power and budgetary authority to the educational institutions themselves.

Whatever one's view of that process, the fact that it has happened has to be accepted, together with the very different educational world in which would-be tutors have to find their way around.

Changes in any system always have positive aspects, at least for some, and it is certainly true that opportunities have been created for freelance teaching and tutoring that were either non-existent or difficult to access previously. Privatisation and the inadequacies of an increasingly under-funded public service also present the entrepreneurial educator and tutor with many more opportunities to provide educational services of all kinds on a businesslike basis for private profit.

This book explores all these opportunities and aims to provide anyone who wants to teach or tutor with help and advice on how to offer their services in a way which will be beneficial to themselves and to their potential students.

If what follows meets those aims, I extend my thanks to all my past colleagues and students who made my time in education both enjoyable and rewarding, as well as to my wife Sue, who has taught me more than she will ever realise.

John T. Wilson

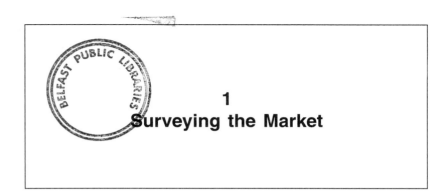

1
Surveying the Market

At a time when many employers are arguing that a national minimum wage set at £4 an hour would wreck British industry and the economy generally, making good money from teaching your skills to others makes a lot of sense.

It is not so long ago that teaching was considered a poorly paid profession (many in education would still argue that they are poorly paid for their professional skills) but now, with the demise of Wages Councils and the vanquishing of the power of trade unions, the kind of money that teaching still commands is often looked at with envy by those outside the profession.

This book will show you how you can earn a great deal more than the national minimum wage – whatever that might be set at – by teaching your skills to others in a variety of ways, all of which are within the reach of the person of average intelligence who has a skill to teach and an enthusiasm for their subject.

Don't worry if you have never done any teaching or instructing before – the following chapters will supply you with all the skills you will need.

CASHING IN ON LEARNING

Learning new skills

Learning new things and acquiring new skills has never been more important than in the present 'Information Age', whether it is coping with computers, improving DIY techniques, job-hunting skills, doing your own income tax returns, learning to run a small business from home or learning a language to work abroad.

So, whatever skills and knowledge you have, you can be certain that somebody, somewhere, wants to share it. You can teach it to them and earn more money than you ever imagined you could earn from such a simple, pleasurable activity.

How much can you earn?

What can you earn from your skills? The answer depends very much on what these skills are, how much in demand they are and how and where you sell them in the education marketplace. You are unlikely to sell your skills in the private marketplace for less than £6 or £7 an hour, while part-time teachers on university-level courses are currently paid around £23 an hour – that's about £140 for a six-hour day or two weekly sessions of three hours. Beyond that, of course are the 'super-stars' of the conference circuit, famous because of their published books, who can earn thousands of pounds for an hour or so's speaking engagement!

MATCHING YOUR SKILLS WITH NEEDS

Assessing your skills

Your first step to becoming a successful freelance tutor is to assess the skills and knowledge that you have to offer and see how these match the learning needs that people have. It may be that what you see as your main expertise is not something that you can readily find an opening for. While almost any knowledge or skill can find a market of people who want to learn some aspect of it (a butcher, for example, could teach others about the various cuts of meat, how to choose them and what to do with them for the best results) there may be little call for a course on nuclear physics.

Finding your hidden skills

Bear in mind, however, two things: first that almost every subject has some aspect of it which is of interest to others and, second, that you probably have secondary knowledge or skills which may be even more marketable than your main skill. These may come from a hobby or interest (woodwork, rock climbing, cooking), community involvement (running meetings, being a school governor) or from life experience (coping with divorce, working abroad, running your own business).

THE SCOPE FOR FREELANCE TUTORING

Life-long learning

Education used to be seen as what happened during the ten to thirteen years you spent in school. Now, however, we talk about 'life-long learning' as the pattern most appropriate for an increasingly complex world in which things change rapidly as new knowledge and information become available every day. The person who ceases to learn, ceases to survive. The need for teachers and tutors of all sorts of things has never been more evident.

What do people want to learn?

Learning needs cover an immense range of subjects, focusing around the areas of work, leisure, family, relationships, physical skills, finance, health, personal growth and curiosity about the world. Just look at the following list for a sample of the things people want to learn about:

acupuncture	music
bath renovating	natural remedies
car maintenance	office skills
computing	psychology
dowsing	quantity surveying
embroidery	relaxation
French	success
gardening	travel
guitar	ukulele
herbs	vegetarianism
income tax	writing
jam-making	Christmas decorations
keeping bees	Yiddish
lapidary	zoology

Where and how do people learn?

Learning can take place in all sorts of places and circumstances such as:

- personal tuition in private homes

- small group tuition in private homes or elsewhere

- formal teaching in schools

- being an instructor in schools

- lecturing in further education colleges

- tutoring an adult education class

- training groups in company premises

- informal tuition in youth clubs

- talks and demonstrations to clubs and organisations

- distance learning by correspondence course
- in practical situations such as workshops or outdoors.

THE SYSTEM AND HOW IT WORKS

Broadly speaking there are five areas where freelance tutors can work:

- in state schools
- in private schools
- in other educational establishments
- in the commercial training field
- as a private tutor.

Let's look at these areas and see how the system works and what opportunities it offers.

State schools

When we think of teaching we invariably think of schools first, and that can be a bit daunting for several reasons. First, our own experience of school may not have been a pleasurable one, particularly if we are in an older age group. However, things have changed considerably – certainly since I was at school – and you may find schools much more relaxed and friendly places than you remember them. Second, you may feel that schools offer you no opportunity for freelance teaching and tutoring as you do not have the qualifications which are, broadly speaking, a four-year teacher training course or a university degree or equivalent, followed by a year's teacher training.

You can, however, become an **instructor** in schools without having these qualifications if you have a skill or a subject to teach which is not covered by the more conventional teaching subjects. You might, for example, become an instructor in hairdressing or beauty care as part of pupils' self-presentation, or your skills as a retired policeman could enable you to teach road safety to young children or roadcraft to young motorcyclists as part of the school's programme. Instructors and unqualified teachers are paid less than qualified teachers, but the rate of pay is still good at between £8.60 and £13.65 an hour.

For those who are trained teachers but have been out of the system for some time there are increasing opportunities to earn as a **freelance teacher**, particularly if there is a shortage of teachers in your subject area. Areas in which there are shortages currently include maths and science, but there may be local shortages which make your particular subjects invaluable. Make enquiries at your local education authority (LEA) office about both supply teaching and part-time posts. Currently rates of pay for part-time teaching are between £60 and £165 per day.

Private schools

Private schools (usually, confusingly, called 'public schools') are not subject to the same constraints as those in the state sector as far as having fully qualified teachers is concerned. This means that while many of the better schools (not necessarily the same thing as the best known schools) have very highly qualified staff, many have a more open policy and may take on people with a degree or simlar qualification who have not done teacher training. In fact there will be people working in this sector with very limited qualifications indeed, whose qualities may lie in their practical skills or professional knowledge. You will usually have to apply directly to the school concerned. See Chapter 5 for more guidance on looking for such work.

Other educational establishments

The further and higher education sectors are, like the private school sector, less limited by the need for formal teaching qualifications, though training schemes are now widespread for both full- and part-time staff. It is still common, however, for someone with the requisite skills to teach a particular subject to be taken on with the proviso that they are willing to undertake some basic training in teaching skills and approaches. This is particularly the case in **adult education**, as the extremely wide range of courses in this sector means that new courses and new tutors are constantly being sought and recruited. This is the most versatile and open of all the areas of state provision and one well worth concentrating on to begin with – particularly if your subject is a bit out of the ordinary.

Consider, too, the needs of the **youth service** and other non-statutory youth clubs, where, like adult education, a wide range of courses is on offer and an informal approach to learning more likely. Many special schools and establishments, both state and private, for people with **special needs** will often consider people less academically qualified provided they have the right personal attitudes and an aptitude for the very special nature of the work.

The commercial training field

Business and commercial training is a wide open field, some of it taking place in employers' premises and some provided independently with attendees either paying for the course themselves or having the bill picked up by their employer.

Work of this kind earns extremely good money indeed, as the average price of a day's training is around £150. Clearly, if you were to run such training courses as a private trainer for commercial firms, you could do very nicely out of ten participants each paying (or their firms paying) £300 for a two-day course. Even allowing for the cost of providing the location and marketing and other expenses, these two days are likely to bring you in considerably more than £1,000 net income.

Additionally training is provided for both employees and the unemployed through **Training and Enterprise Councils** in association with a host of private training agencies. These courses will be predominantly aimed at the job-seeker and will focus on job-search skills, information technology and starting up a small business enterprise. Rates of pay working for these organisations are unlikely to be high when compared with those providing more high-powered managerial courses for companies.

Private tutoring

Offering tuition as a private tutor is for those who like the idea of being totally in control of their own work. While teaching for an organisation, be it commercial or part of the state sector, means that all you have to do is turn up and teach what is required to a ready-assembled group, when you run your own tutoring set-up you have to do everything – advertising, interviewing students, collecting the fees and doing the teaching as well. However, it does have many advantages, chief among them being:

- setting your own fees

- selecting the students you want to work with

- working as many or as few hours as you want to

- teaching to your own syllabus rather than one imposed externally

- developing the business by taking on other tutors

- working from the comfort of your own home

- being able to set expenses against your overall income.

FILLING THE GAPS

Like any business, the teaching and tutoring field is a very competitive one, particularly between institutions as they are forced more and more to act as if they were commercial businesses. There is also competition between tutors for the limited number of teaching posts available.

This can work to your advantage, as you can suggest a course using your skills to an institution not offering your subject who might want to do so to compete with another institution. You can also offer new courses, looking carefully to see what subjects are already covered and tailoring your offering to be just that bit different. While other courses offer 'Dressmaking', you could offer 'Dress Like a Fashion Model for Half the Price of a High Street Outfit' or 'Turn Your Old Clothes into Stunning Fashion Garments'.

Modern marketing is very much niche marketing – looking for a need and then filling it. Think about how you can do this with the subject or skills you have to teach. Later, in Chapter 2, you will find how to assess what it is you have to offer (more than you are probably aware of) and in Chapters 6 and 7 you will be shown how to market yourself and your skills successfully.

BENEFITING FROM RECENT DEVELOPMENTS

Growth of part-timers

A number of recent developments have opened up new opportunities you may be able to benefit from. Among these are the financial pressures which have caused many schools to shed experienced staff whose skills and abilities have to be replaced by cheaper alternatives – this could be you, as a part-time tutor or as a lower (but still adequately) paid instructor.

The National Curriculum

The development of the National Curriculum for schools, with its clear statement of objectives and stages, has opened up opportunities for those who take the trouble to study its requirements and make sure that what they have to offer meets some of the needs outlined for the various stages.

Updating skills

The speed of change affecting many areas of working and personal life make new demands on ordinary people who need to do some learning in order to survive. These might include areas like divorce, computers, self-confidence, interview skills or sales skills, all of which create many opportunities which are capable of being addressed in specially structured courses or by individual tuition. Consider carefully how you might be able to meet some of these needs, for they are the learning needs of the future that are not always addressed by conventional educational institutions.

CASE STUDIES

Linda puts jam on her bread
Housewife Linda used to grow and collect fruit to make jam to provide her family with high quality produce. When her family grew up she found she was still making jam in quantities she and her husband simply could not get through themselves, so she started selling it at the local Womens Institute market. Despite a relatively high selling price, once she had counted her costs she reckoned she was making only 15p a jar, which worked out at roughly £3 an hour for her labour. A friend suggested she approached the local adult education centre with a course on jam making and she now earns about five times as much teaching others how to make their own jam.

They pay this marine sergeant to bawl at them!
Tom, an ex-Royal Marine sergeant, couldn't find a job that challenged him in the way army life had. After a succession of unsatisfactory and poorly paid jobs he decided to sell his house and invest the proceeds together with his army gratuity and savings to buy a small hotel in the Lake District. He runs this hotel as his own outdoor pursuits centre where he is able to use the skills he had learned in the army to help others develop themselves physically and mentally.

Elaine and Eddie decide to run a portfolio business
Redundant teachers Elaine and Eddie use their skills and expertise to run a 'portfolio business, taking in supply teaching and their own private tutorial agency. Because of the tax advantages of running a small business they are now earning more money for less work than they did as full-time teachers.

CHECKLIST

1. Teaching rates can vary from £6 or £7 an hour to £23 per hour and more. What is the minimum amount you are willing to accept as an hourly rate?

2. Remember that you probably have more skills to offer than are immediately obvious. Chapter 2 shows you how to begin assessing your skills. Why not make a list of the ones you can think of immediately and add to it as more occur to you?

3. The ways in which teaching and learning take place are amazingly varied. Which can you think of that might be a starting point for you?

4. You don't have to be a qualified teacher to help people to learn, though a willingness to acquire some basic teaching skills will help. Why not ask at your local college what short courses there are in this area?

5. Look around your neighbourhood. What institutions exist? What learning needs are there which may not be being met?

6. If you are a qualified teacher, why not contact your local education authority to enquire about shortage subjects, supply teaching, part-time teaching and other opportunities?

7. Get the prospectuses of your local college, adult education centre and other institutions. What is on offer? What is missing? Can you spot gaps in the market?

8. Have you contacted the youth service to see if they need instructors in your subject or skill area?

9. Try to assess the likely training needs of local business and industry which may relate to your expertise.

10. Scan the classified ads and shop window cards to see what private tuition is on offer. Is there room for what you have to offer?

11. What new learning needs can you see emerging? Can you meet any of them?

2
Assessing Your Skills

If you have got as far as reading to this point you must have some confidence that you may have something to offer, however tentatively, as a freelance teacher or tutor. In this chapter you are invited to explore more thoroughly what it is that you may have to offer. It is likely to be more than you think.

You have probably focused on the skills you have which are most obvious and those, for most people, stem from their jobs. So an accountant might think of teaching business accounts, a beautician will feel confident of offering classes in beauty care and a retired policeman may be keen to promote an understanding of home and personal security.

YOU AND YOUR SKILLS

Are you missing out on your potential?

To limit yourself in this way, however, is possibly to miss out on a great deal of additional potential which most of us have. This can be illustrated by the story of a redundant storeman who was a regular attender at the unemployment drop-in centre operated at the adult education centre I used to run. My staff encouraged him to think of his experience and interests outside of work and he talked with some enthusiasm of his years as a scout master. It was at this point that it began to dawn on him that he could think of a job change to a more interesting and fulfilling career in the Youth Service for which his spare-time scouting experience suited him. Unfortunately, within days of this conversation a storeman's job came up unexpectedly and he took it, missing out on a new and probably more satisfying career!

Your skills are transferable

What this story demonstrates is that skills are transferable. In other words, the skills and aptitudes that you have acquired and use in one area of your life, whether at work, in leisure pursuits or spare-time interests, are available for you to use in a new situation. If you are a competent housewife you could run a residential home, for example, or your sympathetic nature and listening skills could be the foundation, with further training, for becoming a counsellor.

Looking at yourself and your skills

Plato ascribed the words carved on the temple of Apollo at Delphi, 'Know thyself', to the Seven Wise Men, but wiser still are those who can see themselves objectively enough to be successful in the quest for self-knowledge!

When you are looking at yourself as objectively as you can, don't forget to consider and note those things other than skills that also have value to you as a potential freelance tutor – **personal qualities** such as patience, a sense of humour, being a good listener (teaching is very far from being all talking!) or confidence in talking to and dealing with others. Qualities such as tact, intelligence, determination, tolerance or forthrightness are worth listing, together with qualities of which you may be less proud, such as short-temperedness, being shy, inability to tolerate fools gladly, or laziness. It is just as important to know the down side as well as the positive attributes that you can bring to the teaching process!

Most people, however, are more likely to be only too well aware of their deficiencies, real or imagined, when it comes to assessing their potential for the new role of freelance tutor. That is only natural, for launching out on something new and relatively unknown is always challenging and, perhaps, a little threatening.

Overcoming unhelpful modesty

While it is good to be aware of your limitations as well as assessing your strengths so that you avoid arrogance and overconfidence, it is unhelpful to be over-modest when carrying out an assessment of your skills.

Scientists tell us that we use only a tiny fraction of the awesome power of our brains and it is the same with our skills and abilities in general. Most people know a great deal more than they are aware of and have a wide and impressive range of skills and achievements gathered over years of experience and learning. You are no exception, and it will surprise you how many hidden skills and abilities you can list once you begin to follow the skills-assessment techniques given below.

ASSESSING YOURSELF WITH SOME SIMPLE QUESTIONS

Looking at your achievements

Sit down with a piece of paper and try this very simple exercise in surveying your many achievements. Ask yourself the eight questions in Figure 1 and write down the answers in lists that you can (and will!) add to as you suddenly remember more things later in the day (or week, or month).

Looking for the less obvious

What you are doing in exploring the below questions is increasing your objective awareness of who and what you are, what you know and what value your experiences have. You should end up listing all the jobs and occupations you have ever had, your hobbies, interests, qualifications, skills, experiences, knowledge you have acquired along the way and all the organisations and causes you have taken part in and supported over the years.

You are looking for the less obvious aspects of your life, hidden

---

1. What subject/job/professional skills do I possess?
2. What skills have I acquired while doing my job? (A teacher will have acquired management skills, a bank manager will have interviewing and advisory skills – or should have! A hairdresser will have developed listening and conversational skills and so on.)
3. What part-time jobs have I done throughout my life?
4. What community/voluntary activities or projects have I taken part in?
5. What personal problems or difficulties have I overcome in my life and what skills or knowledge have I gained as a result?
6. What courses have I studied throughout my life?
7. What skills and knowledge have I acquired through my hobbies and spare-time interests?
8. What new or difficult thing have I done or learned recently? (For example, built a garden wall, learned to operate a computer, sorted out a friend's problem, negotiated a union deal etc.)

Fig. 1. Looking at your achievements.

skills and abilities which others may well see, but which you are too close to even to be aware that you have them and that they are significant and of value to others as well as to yourself.

You will find, as your list grows, a picture of yourself emerging in which you will see yourself with new eyes, and new possibilities will open up in all sorts of directions.

Identifying your skills

Ask yourself in what general areas your skills lie. This seems an obvious question, the answer lying in the job or profession you do. What you need to do, however, is to look below the surface of that professional description and see what core skills lie at the heart of, for example, being a dentist or an estate agent or a mother and housewife. Look for generic skills by breaking down what you do in your job and in other areas of your life so that you begin to build up a rounded and detailed picture of the whole range of skills that you have. Some of these you will use so naturally that you will not even think of them as skills and others will be less obvious because you have never stopped to analyse just what it is you do and what you are good at.

Look at the list in Figure 2 and ask yourself in which of the areas your skills lie. Follow the same listing procedure as you did in considering your achievements. Take each area in turn and think of ways in which things in your life and experience can be described in these terms. Add to the list other areas which you think of as you carry out this assessment. As you list examples under each heading you will build up a profile that will begin to indicate the broad areas where your skills lie. The result may surprise you.

More questions to ask about your skills

Ask yourself the following questions without supplying the most obvious answers. One of the best ways to do this is to answer quickly without pausing to think. The answers may sometimes surprise you or give you sudden enlightenment or insight. Write them down.

1. What skills do you consider your strengths?

2. What areas do you think you are weak in?

3. Which of the skill areas you have listed do you most enjoy doing?

4. Would you like to develop any of these skills further?

5. Are there new skills you would like to explore?

Do your skills lie within:		**Examples**
arts/artistic	☐	
design	☐	
driving	☐	
general service	☐	
influencing	☐	
explaining	☐	
managing	☐	
leading/supervising	☐	
making decisions	☐	
literary/writing	☐	
verbal/speaking/listening	☐	
languages	☐	
mechanical/engineering	☐	
making and constructing	☐	
numerical	☐	
financial	☐	
earth-based	☐	
people-based	☐	
paperwork/administration	☐	
practical	☐	
thinking/ideas/critical/planning	☐	
scientific/technical	☐	
social/helping/caring	☐	
problem-solving	☐	

Fig. 2. Identifying your skills.

WHY YOU DON'T NEED TO BE AN 'EXPERT'

If you think you need to be an expert before you can teach, think
again. What is an expert? An expert is someone who is so close to
their subject that they can't explain it to ordinary mortals. An expert
is someone who knows so much that they no longer know what mat-
ters. An expert is someone who knows six things you don't know.
Experts, in a word, usually make very poor teachers and tutors: their
expertise too often gets in the way.

Computer experts are a very clear example of this. Years ago, when
personal computers were just coming in (and primitive beasts they
were too!) I had great difficulty in finding computer tutors to help

ordinary people come to terms with computers and what they could do for them. I would go into the computer class and find a whole class struggling to write computer programmes in computer code. Three or four weeks later there were only a few persevering students left. The keen computer tutor – an 'expert' – had driven away all those ordinary people who only wanted to know what computers were about and what they could do with them. They were certainly not interested in writing computer programmes. Someone who knew less about computers but used them in their life would have made a far better tutor than the computer 'expert', for all their knowledge. You see, sometimes knowledge can get in the way of learning!

What you need, to be to be a good freelance tutor or teacher, is the ability to understand what other people want or need to know about a subject and the ability to help them to learn it for themselves. In later chapters we will explore this role and show you how easy it is to carry it out.

RECOGNISING YOUR UNIQUE CONTRIBUTION

You are a unique human being. There has never been, in all the history of the world with its billions and billions of people, anyone exactly like you, with your attributes, your unique mind-set, your experiences, your individual body of knowledge. You have something of value to offer to others as a freelance tutor and teacher. All you have to do, is to find it. And if you have followed the exercises in this chapter you should be starting to identify the various areas where you may have a contribution to make.

FINDING THE SECRET OF ABSOLUTE CONFIDENCE

Maybe you don't know enough to run a three-year degree course in a subject, but does that matter? No, it doesn't, because there are plenty of people – the majority of people, in fact – whose needs are for a much more limited learning experience. Perhaps you could begin by offering a one-day school or a five-week workshop on the area of your chosen subject which you feel most confident about. Begin small.

Realise, too, that teaching is not about having to know everything – you will always come across someone who knows a lot more than you do. Later in this book you will be shown how to deal with this and other teaching situations. The secret of absolute confidence is to adopt the attitude that you are there to share with other people, and to help them to share with each other, the knowledge and enthusiasm you all have about a particular aspect of being a human being in this exciting period of human history. Relax and enjoy it – and they will too!

CASE STUDIES

Linda swapped physiotherapy for jam sessions
Linda trained initially as a physiotherapist and left the health service to have a family. Later, with the children grown up a little, she wanted something to do to earn money towards the growing expenses of their schooling and leisure activities. She sat down and thought about how to earn without going back to work in hospitals, the nearest one being thirteen miles away. She began by developing her jam-making skills and selling locally, then realised from buyers' remarks that others would like to learn to make their own jams successfully. Her hobby has become her job and she says she enjoys teaching more than she enjoyed doing physiotherapy.

To the hills with the Marines
It was only after suffering a succession of unsatisfactory jobs that Tom, ex-Marine sergeant, began to realise that none of the skills he had developed as a soldier were being used. He didn't, however, want to return to army life, even if that were possible. Reading of a special management centre in Wales which specialised in running activity-based management courses, he realised that this was the perfect way for him to use his own skills in the same area and set about finding a place in the Lakes to run similar courses. He also found that during his army career he had developed the management and administration skills his new venture also needed.

Eddie and Elaine expand their skills portfolio
Having set up their own tutorial agency together with supply teaching to capitalise on their professional skills, Eddie and his partner Elaine realised that their skills in dealing with people coupled with their teaching skills, equipped them to add a distributorship with a nutritional health products company to their portfolio of earning activities. Their success in this new venture depends on introducing new distributors and training them in the business. They have discovered that the hidden skills of teaching can be transferred effectively to selling.

CHECKLIST

1. You need to get to know yourself more objectively in terms of your skills and aptitudes without being over-modest about what you have to offer. Start thinking about this.

2. Your skills are transferable. Once you have begun to identify your skills, start thinking about other situations in which you could put them to use.

3. Give some thought to your personal qualities, identifying those that will help you to become a tutor and those which are less desirable in teaching. Will teaching and tutoring suit you as a person?

4. You have more skills and abilities than you possibly realise. Work through the techniques in this chapter so that you begin to identify your achievements and your skills and pin-point the ones you particularly enjoy or are good at. Those are the areas to focus on for your role as a freelance tutor and teacher.

5. Remember, you don't have to be an 'expert'. The skill of a good teacher is to manage other people's learning, not to be a 'know-all'.

3
Teaching and Learning

THE DIFFERENCE BETWEEN TEACHING AND LEARNING

People often talk about teaching and learning as if they are the same thing. They are not. They are very different.

Look at it this way – little Johnny spends eleven years at school being taught by professional teachers. He leaves school barely able to scrawl his own name and address on a piece of paper and finds reading the *Sun* newspaper intellectually demanding. He has been taught – but has he learned anything?

On the other hand, little Jeannie spends a great deal of time at home and in hospital because of a drawn-out childhood illness. She is seldom at school and as a result gets very little teaching. Yet at the age of sixteen she devours books of all kinds, does a lot of writing on a computer and is secretary of a national association for young people with her illness. She has not been taught – but my goodness she has been doing some learning!

Therein lies a lesson for you in your aspirations to become a freelance tutor or teacher. You can teach until you are blue in the face, but you have no guarantee that those you teach will learn anything.

HOW DID YOU LEARN?

In fact – and here is a strange thing to read in a book about how to become a freelance tutor – most people's valuable learning happens outside formal learning situations. How did you learn to speak such good English (or whatever is your first language)? Certainly not at school. Certainly not because your parents sat down and 'taught' you. You learned, as every other human being does, by absorbing speech, by imitation and a gradual understanding of what it all means.

How did you learn to ride a bike? Who taught you to play football or put on lipstick? How do you know how to walk? Where did you discover how to make relationships with the opposite sex? Did your love of your favourite music come from a study course?

The point is that you learn most things without being taught them formally. This doesn't mean, of course, that all teaching is a waste of time, though a great deal of it in schools is, because school pupils are forced to go to school and most don't want to learn a great deal of what is taught there. Teaching only works properly when people want to learn – and even then it will only work if it is focused strongly on students learning, rather than teachers teaching.

FOCUSING ON THE LEARNER NOT THE TEACHER

The key, then, to good teaching is that it focuses on the learning process and the needs and interests of the learner. If you are teaching car maintenance you will find that most people will be impatient with your introductory lecture on the history of the automobile and will be turned off by your learned explanations of the complex chemistry and physics of burning gas within the chambers of the internal combustion engine. They want to know where the ignition timer is and how to set it properly. They want to be shown how to clean the carburettor or dismantle the gearbox. They know what they want from the education process – but do *you* know what they want? And are you prepared to give it to them?

TEACHING OR ENTERTAINING?

I used to visit my classes when I was principal of a large adult education centre. I'd chat to the students and they would sometimes tell me what a wonderful tutor they had and how stimulating and enjoyable the lesson was.

'What was it about?' I'd ask.
'Well', they would say slowly, 'it was about the Egyptians.'
'Yes?' I would prompt.
'Well, it was . . . um . . . well he told us all about them. It was fascinating . . . the pyramids and all that, you know . . .'

I didn't. So I asked, what, exactly had been so spellbinding. All I got was more protestations about how wonderful the young historian was, how much he knew, how interesting it had all been. It was clear that, however entertaining the lecture on the Egyptians and the pyramids had been, the students had actually not retained very much more than a vague impression of magnificence. In fact, they had not learned very much at all.

Have the students learned anything?

If there is a difference between teaching and learning, there is also a distinct difference between teaching and entertainment. Yet many intelligent people believe that they are very much the same thing. They believe that if you can entertain people for forty-five minutes by a clever and colourful account of some aspect of their subject so that people find it pleasurable, then they have been doing a great teaching job.

Not so. There is only one test of teaching. Have the students learned anything? Teaching as entertainment is like throwing mud against the wall. Some of it will stick, but not very much. And it won't be there next week, that's for sure.

Of course teaching should be interesting, but if you want applause take up amateur dramatics. If you want to be a good teacher you will have to forego the pleasure of being the star of the show. You are not the star of the show – the students are and their learning will depend on their performance more than on yours. And it should be their performance which is applauded rather than yours as teacher.

DO YOU WANT TO BE BRILLIANT?

Another popular myth about the good teacher that needs to be shattered is the image of the sparkling mind or the consummate craftsman demonstrating his superior brain power or innate skill to a group of admiring and appreciative students stunned by the brilliance of their tutor – a god amongst mere mortals.

That kind of teaching amounts to not much more than showing off. Again it is putting a focus on the teacher and how clever he or she is and not on the learning needs of the student. While it is important that your students know that you have a sufficient grasp of the subject, it is, in fact, dispiriting and off-putting for the students to be shown just what a big gap there is between the breadth and depth of the tutor's understanding and their own, scarcely existing knowledge.

The object of the exercise is not to demonstrate how clever you are as a tutor, but to help them learn in an atmosphere of support and mutual respect. Bear that in mind and avoid the tendency to show just how clever you are and you will win more respect than any show-off who is effectively teaching students to devalue themselves.

THE SECRET OF BEING A GOOD TEACHER

The secret of being a good teacher is less about how much you know or how skilled you are, and more about having an empathy with other people and an ability to understand and respect their needs as learners.

When people come away from your classes and workshops with an increased understanding of the subject, a greater ability to do what you do or more confidence in their ability to make progress and put their new skills to work, then you will have become a good teacher.

PRACTISING STUDENT-CENTRED LEARNING

The approach known as **student-centred learning** is not a difficult concept, more an attitude of mind and a willingness to find practices that enhance that approach. It means, simply, putting the students and their needs at the heart of the process with the teaching being hand-maid to the learning experience.

While students' needs will vary a great deal, as will the knowledge and experience they bring to your subject, there are some fairly simple and perhaps obvious things you can do to make sure that you at least start off with a student-centred approach.

Finding out their learning needs

At the start of any teaching or course of study make it your first task, after making the students welcome and at ease, to find out what it is that they want to learn. Try to think, and to get them to think, in terms of **doing** – 'What is it you want to be able to **do** that you can't do now?' is an excellent starting point.

Once you have found out what your students want (and they won't all want the same thing – but more of how to tackle that later) you will be in a better position to plan a course that will actually achieve that – and, believe me, that is more unusual than you might think among teachers!

Setting appropriate goals

What is being suggested here is that you adopt a goal-centred approach to teaching and learning. Most teachers have goals of a sort. They come to a class with the idea that by the end of it the students will have in their heads a good bit of the knowledge of their subject that they (the teachers) have in their heads. So the French tutor gets stuck into grammar and structure and pluperfect tenses and lists of verbs that take the subjunctive and all sorts of baffling and frustrating concepts. All the students wanted was to be able to ask the way to the hotel and the price of a cup of coffee – but the tutor didn't know that because she hadn't bothered to find out. She wasn't student-centred but tutor or subject-centred. Or to put it another way – self-centred.

But your teaching, student-centred because you have asked the students what they want to learn, will be much more successful.

Being specific

Be specific in finding out what the students want to learn – or, more exactly, make sure that *they* are specific. A goal needs to be specific if there is to be any hope of achieving it. If your students express their aims as 'to learn French' or 'to become proficient in woodwork' or some other vague or all-embracing notion, get them to be more specific. Ask them what they want to be able to say in French by the end of the course. Ask what, exactly, they want to make out of wood by the end of the first term.

Negotiating goals

You may, of course, need to negotiate your students' goals if they seem too ambitious. For someone who has never done any singing to aim at taking the lead part in next year's amateur operatic society's opera is, to say the least, a trifle ambitious. Unless they are exceptional, they are likely to be disappointed without your negotiating with them a more realistic and achievable goal. That is part of your job as a student-centred tutor.

Meeting different needs

By the time you have noted your students' aims in the first lesson you may be in despair as to how you can possibly meet more than a dozen quite different and unrelated goals. That's where you need to learn some effective teaching methods which will help you to cope with this and other aspects of teaching, whether in groups or on a one-to-one basis. Some guidance on coping with the wide variety of students' abilities and goals will also be given in the next chapter.

UNDERSTANDING HOW PEOPLE LEARN

Before you decide how you are going to teach and what methods are likely to be effective, you must first have some idea of how people learn.

Not just knowledge

It is important to understand that learning is not just related to knowledge and information. The most important kind of learning is an empowering experience – it enables us to do things we could not do before. That is the touchstone of learning – what changes have occurred? What can you do which you could not do before you had the learning experience? Learning is identified with change: change in knowledge, change in understanding or awareness, change in skills or change in behaviour. Learning is identifiable: look out for it.

We might define learning, then, as **changes in understanding and behaviour brought about by particular experiences**. These experiences may be random experiences that come our way in the natural flow of life or they may be planned experiences designed by ourselves or others so that learning can take place – '**learning experiences**' in fact, which is perhaps a more useful phrase to use than 'teaching', 'lessons', or 'course', because it keeps to the forefront the actual result we want to achieve: that people learn things.

It is fairly obvious too, as has been already pointed out, that learning is different from teaching. Teaching is the activity carried out by a teacher or instructor – talking, demonstrating, answering questions, asking questions, leading discussion or whatever – while learning is what the students, or individuals on their own, are doing. Learning is an active process and the major responsibility for success is the learner's. That concept is fundamental to teaching adults – or, indeed, anyone.

In a learning experience what is it that people are learning? Is it a subject, or is it a process? Of course, it is both, but it is important to move away from the notion of learning in 'subjects' to the notion of learning as meeting the real needs of people. What is also very important is that the kind of teaching you adopt helps people to continue to learn by themselves – that you teach them to become learners.

Learning parrot-fashion

The oldest model of learning most of us have is rote learning, the method by which we remember formulae, pieces of poetry that stay with us until senile dementia sets in (or alternatively, which we forget until our deteriorating brains unlock the brain cells containing these learned memories) or other factual formulations. Clearly this has its place and we all use it when we want to remember how many days there are in July or what nine articles at eight pounds each come to.

Memory techniques

Other forms of memory-based learning are also useful in many areas, particularly those based on remembering disconnected information or in the earlier stages of language learning. We use various memory devices and techniques for these in addition to the repetitions of rote learning. If we have a visual imagination we may remember names by conjuring up visual images.

For example, in the study of psychology we might want to remember that the hippocampal is an organ of the brain which, if damaged, causes the loss of recent short-term memory. You might visualise a hippopotamus (hippo) in a tent (camp) who is called A1 (al) and is scratching his head.

There are techniques involving the grouping of words, rhythms, associations and, probably more efficient than memory 'tricks', the proper organisation of material to be learned into patterns that are meaningful to you.

Using the senses

Learning, however, isn't just about absorbing information – and it is a fairly complicated process. Put at its simplest, it involves:

• **listening**
• **seeing** (and, sometimes, smelling and tasting)
• **doing**
• **sharing** and
• **understanding**

not necessarily all of them at the same time or in that order. How can this shape our teaching so that learning occurs?

The Chinese, who discovered practically everything before anyone else, summed it up in a simple proverb (didn't they always?):

'I hear and I forget
            I see and I remember
                        I do and I understand.'

Talk to your students all you like; just remember, fascinated as they may be, they will probably forget most of your words of wisdom.

Show your students pictures, posters, objects and demonstrations;

since vision accounts for something like 80 per cent of the information we take in, the chances are that they will remember more.

Get your students **doing** the activity, be it carving a clothes peg, making a cake or speaking Italian, and you stand the greatest chance of them actually learning what you have set out to teach them, for they will be **involved**, they will be **motivated**, they will be **sharing** in the experience of whatever it is that you are teaching, and **they will be learning**.

People will learn. You can't stop them. It is an inevitable part of living and growing. What *you* can do is to hinder or, on the other hand, help them to learn from you the skills and knowledge you want to share with them. If you follow the principles discussed in this chapter and summarised in Figure 3, you will experience the joy of helping others to learn and that is much more satisfying than giving an impressive performance which has little to do with your students learning.

- Creating an environment in which it will be easy to learn.

- Setting up situations which will lead to learning taking place.

- Providing resources (including yourself) to aid the learning.

- Knowing what it is the students require to learn.

- Guiding the students in the learning process.

- Being aware of the difficulties the students face.

- Providing for the students' differing learning needs.

- Encouraging the students and giving them confidence.

- Helping students to assess and evaluate their own learning.

- Giving the students a sense of achievement.

- Directing students in exploring their further learning needs.

Fig. 3. The tutor's role.

TEACHING AND TUTORING METHODS

What follows is by no means an exhaustive summary of recognised teaching methods and there is only space for a very brief description of each one. You may come across other approaches or devise your own which may work better for you. The key to successful practice is variety – try to use several different methods during each teaching session whether teaching one person or a group.

Lectures and talks

The old-fashioned 'chalk and talk' has its place – but a small one. If you are going to talk to the whole class, keep it short and break it up with a change of activity. Once you are relaxed and experienced enough, use questions and discussion as part of a lecture or talk presentation. Involvement is the key to interest – and don't forget that the effective attention span for the average person is about 15–20 minutes. Using illustrations such as posters, slides, models etc. will make any talk-based teaching more interesting and effective.

If using this method use it sparingly, speak from notes and look at your audience. If you use a blackboard or whiteboard don't talk with your back to the students while writing on the board (they won't hear you). Remember too that as people get older they can't see to read the board very well and their hearing is less acute, so make sure there aren't barriers like that getting in the way of learning.

Discussion

This is one of the most involving methods of teaching, provided your students are relaxed enough to say something and it is conducted with some planning. What is the purpose of the discussion? Is it simply to exchange views and arguments? How much are you as tutor going to control it and get involved in the argument? Consider setting guidelines for any discussion such as not getting personal, accepting criticism, not interrupting, proper listening, getting people to summarise what someone has said before commenting and so on.

Questions

This is one of the most effective methods for getting people to think. You can use it in a variety of ways, such as asking questions of individuals within the group, putting questions up for general comment, asking a series of ever more probing questions and so on. Remember that the point of questions is to help students think through an issue or problem, not to put them on the spot or make them feel inadequate, nor for you to show how dumb they are and how smart you are for knowing the answers. Don't be afraid to ask questions you don't know the answers to or be afraid to admit it. You are on a learning quest together. Remember to give praise and encouragement (but don't be patronising).

Demonstration

This is obviously more appropriate to some subjects, notably the more practical subjects. Show how to pronounce the language, how to use the saw, how to prepare the salad or whatever. Do avoid the mistake of boring the pants off everyone by giving long, drawn out demonstrations that don't give anyone a chance to follow up by practising it themselves. Adapt the Blue Peter style of preparing your demonstration beforehand so that you can show the most in the shortest space of time – 'This is one I prepared earlier'.

Exercises

The natural follow on from demonstration is to get students to do exercises that take them some way towards being able to do the complete thing – whatever it is. Try to make them easy, graded and fun. Give the students feedback on their performance so that they can learn by the experience and get it right. A sense of achievement is important, so give generous praise – remember, learners are easily discouraged.

Doing

Some radical educational theorists argue that there is no such thing as 'learning' to do something – there is just 'doing' it. This is what the old apprenticeship system was based on, with the apprentice being allowed to do more and more of the job as his skills developed until he was fully competent. While you can take this to extremes, it is good to remember that it is a sounder principle than filling folk with nothing but theory. Remember the Chinese proverb, 'I **do** and I understand.'

Role play

This is a fun way to get insight into human situations. Once he steps into the shoes of a striking factory hand in a simulation or role play of a factory dispute, the managing director may begin to understand more clearly points of view other than his own.

To set up a role play you need to assign roles. Write a brief description of each role on an index card and give them out – 'You are a married factory worker with a young family who doesn't want to strike because you desperately need the money and you are afraid of losing your job' etc. You (more appropriately the person playing the role of the managing director) then announce the situation – 'A fire has meant that part of the factory has had to be shut down and the management are taking the opportunity to lay off half the workforce.' Don't just let them enjoy the play acting – debrief them afterwards and discuss the issues that arose, the feelings they had, how they see the situation. Draw out the general principles that the role play was designed to show.

Case studies
These are very similar in purpose to role plays except that they are descriptions of situations and what took place, what people did, how others reacted and what the result was. These are read through and discussed in terms of the issues and principles that are brought up.

Games
There are a whole range of educational and other games that can be played as part of the learning process. Old-fashioned parlour games can be used to explore lifestyles before television, demonstrate memory skills and so on. Some games demonstrate how conflict arises, how we perceive situations and so on. Use games to make learning fun!

Group work
One of the great fears people have of teaching is that they see it as having to stand in front of people and talk to them for an hour or more at a time without getting stuck for words. Good teaching avoids as much as possible the 'talking at them' approach in favour of creating a variety of learning situations which involve the students more. For one thing, it's less boring and, for another, it's more effective as a learning and teaching strategy.

Working in groups is a very effective way of using the resources of those learning. Try a **whole-class group** by simply rearranging the room in a circle or semi-circle. It's amazing how this breaks down the barriers between tutor and the students. It's easier for them to contribute and the tutor's job becomes one of conducting the group – or to use a jargon word, 'enabling' the group.

Alternatively you can **divide the class up** and **set them work to do** in groups. In this way the students are encouraged to take responsibility for their own learning and are not always looking to the tutor to answer questions or tell them everything. This is the first step towards them becoming capable of independent learning, which should always be the eventual goal of the good tutor.

Groups can be used for **more than just discussion**. They can be used for problem-solving, for practising a foreign language, for doing a task, for discussing without the sometimes inhibiting presence of the tutor. They can report back to the others, which introduces fresh learning skills in marshalling thoughts and arguments and presenting them in an ordered way, reinforcing what they have learned by giving voice to them in this way.

Groups can be **any size** – as small as pairs, but preferably avoiding threes, which seem always to end up as two against one or someone feeling left out or uncomfortable. Five to seven is a good number as a group of this size gives everyone, even those who are shy, the chance to have their say in less intimidating circumstances than the whole class.

Brainstorming

This is a useful way to work with groups where you want to generate as many ideas as possible. It can be done in a large group or by getting people to work in pairs or small groups of four or five. The important thing about brainstorming is that people are encouraged to think up and note down any idea they can think of on the topic under investigation. It doesn't matter if they are silly or crazy ideas – even impossible – and no criticism or adverse comment is allowed during the brainstorming phase. Later the ideas are examined to see if there are the germs of possible solutions even in the crazy ideas.

Supporting and listening

Other useful ways to use small groups are to get students to help each other using their strengths to match another's weaker points, or for small groups to listen carefully to what one person has to say without cutting in and interrupting, then be given the chance to make suggestions or criticisms as appropriate.

Individual work

Another way is for each student to be working on his or her own. While this is a traditional technique in teaching craft skills, it can equally be used in more 'intellectual' areas, where individuals can be asked to write down lists, thoughts, arguments or whatever and then asked to share them with a larger group.

Worksheets

It is a good idea to prepare a number of task or problem-related worksheets which can be used on an individual basis. These can be swapped around and will provide hours of useful work and learning within the overall teaching plan.

Project work

This is a specific technique for working on an individual basis, where each student has a project of their own which they can work on both during the lesson and at home as well. It is a useful way to give variety within a teaching session to allot some time to such work, which also gives the tutor the chance to talk privately to each member of the group to help them with their individual problems or to check progress.

Problem-solving

While problem-solving has been mentioned as a way for groups to be set to work, it is also a whole approach to teaching which works as a general strategy. For example, a new group learning about advertising could be asked to prepare a campaign to advertise a new shop or other business. This would draw from them what they know already as individuals and they would begin to learn from each other. In trying to do this without expert help they would very quickly realise what the problems and difficulties were and what it was that they required to know, which would begin to give the course both direction and meaning.

Discovery learning

This is a 'modern' method of working which is much misunderstood and maligned. It does *not* mean that you just leave your students floundering around to find out everything themselves – after all, the reason they have sought out a teacher or tutor is to benefit from their knowledge and expertise. If the discovery method were simply finding out everything yourself, then there would be little need for education at all.

The value of the discovery method is that, by setting up **thoughtfully designed learning situations**, students experience the basic principles for themselves – it's back to that basic Chinese philosophy that we only truly learn what we experience. Used properly it is very powerful and leads to solid and lasting learning.

LISTENING MORE THAN YOU TALK

Surveying some of these ways of working suggests that good teaching has more to do with listening than with talking. As in life in general, it is good to remember when teaching that we have one mouth and two ears and they should be used in that proportion! The more you listen to the students, the more you will know what their learning needs are and be able to meet them – often by inviting other students to supply the information or the answer. Good teaching (and therefore good learning) is a co-operative endeavour.

CASE STUDIES

Linda's students share in the teaching

When Linda started to teach jam-making courses at the local adult education centre she would prepare extensive lectures and write recipes up on the board for students to write down. She found it exhausting and demanding, especially when trying to fit in a demonstration of jam-making technique as well.

After talking to a more experienced tutor, Linda thought about how she was tackling her teaching and decided to experiment a bit. She tried an evening when she invited the students to bring in their own favourite recipes and the evening was spent in discussing the particular methods that people used. The students liked this as they were able to contribute to other students' knowledge (and to Linda's!) as well as learning from the others.

Now group discussion is a regular feature as well as demonstrations by individual students demonstrating their own methods to the class. Everyone gets a chance to take the limelight and Linda's teaching has become easier as well as more interesting.

Getting to work right away

Tom's early courses began rather stiffly with a regimental-style monologue covering the course and the principles of leadership it was designed to inculcate. That meant that at the end of the Friday evening of a weekend course the most strenuous thing the assembled company had achieved was a swift walk to the local pub.

Tom became aware that people were disappointed to be lectured at instead of getting stuck in. He could hardly take them up the fells on the first evening session, so he did some thinking and devised some tricky problems that had to be solved using limited apparatus among the trees at the bottom of his centre's garden.

Now after dinner a couple of hours of challenging limbering up is put in which whets the appetite of course participants for the more strenuous stuff on the Saturday and Sunday. And the course principles? Discussed with much liveliness at the bar of the local!

Variety is the spice of life in private tutorials

Much of Elaine and Eddie's work is one-to-one tutoring which many students found very demanding. Since their tutorial agency had expanded, with other tutors working on the premises at the same time, they decided to create a different kind of learning experience in which students doing the same subject attend the agency at the same time but for a longer period.

Students initially check in with their own tutor for the first half-hour's review of progress then go into a group situation with another tutor for a twenty-minute group presentation. After a coffee break there is a half-hour of working at prepared worksheets and other exercises before going back to their own tutors to have the work checked and work set to be done over the following week.

CHECKLIST

1. Ask yourself all the time, 'Am I just teaching – or are they learning?'

2. Think about the last new thing you learned to do. How did you learn it? What were the difficulties you experienced in learning it? How did you know when you were successful? Could you measure your learning?

3. When you think about teaching your subject what do you think that the students will be most interested in learning? (Rather than what you think they ought to know.) Can you express these in goals or concrete achievements?

4. Can you define what changes you would want to see in your students after a course of lessons with you? What, specifically, will they be able to do that they couldn't do before coming on the course?

5. Will it bother you that students will only want to learn a limited amount of what you want to teach them? Can you find ways to enable them to achieve their objectives without having to know

everything that you know? What short-cuts can you offer them to help them to do this?

6. How many of the senses can you bring into your teaching of your subject? Be specific about how you would do this.

7. Can you make a list of objects, pictures, posters and other aids you could use to teach your subject?

8. What demonstrations, exercises, role plays, case studies and games could you use to make teaching your subject more involving and interesting for the students?

4
Planning and Running Your Course

TAKING THE RELEVANT FACTORS INTO ACCOUNT

Adopting your own style

However well you know your subject, don't think you can teach it successfully without doing some planning. And don't think you can simply model yourself on those who taught you and do much the same as they did. For one thing, that was likely to have been some years ago and they were probably operating on a model of teaching that was out of date even then! For another, you are not them, and what worked for them may not suit you. You have to look at your own strengths, your own personality and your own particular skills.

Understanding the students' needs

Moreover, you will be taking into account, probably much more than anyone who ever taught you, the needs and difficulties of your students, for you will be a student-centred tutor.

What is simple to you is only so because you know so much. If you are going to teach sailing and think that you just have to get the students in the boat and show them how to do it, you will be surprised how thick they suddenly become! They won't understand it when you tell them to drop the centreboard. They'll be bewildered when you tell them to catch hold of a sheet and pull on it. They will not be able to comprehend what you are actually doing when you come about. And they won't learn.

What you have to do is to try to put yourself into their shoes – imagine the depths of their initial ignorance. It is difficult, because it will probably have been a long time since you felt like they do and you probably can't remember it. What you will have to do is to try to analyse all the skills and knowledge you take for granted and break it down into very simple, understandable concepts and stages that students can begin to absorb bit by bit.

Keeping the authorities happy

Even if you are doing private tutoring on a one-to-one basis you will have to look beyond the student to others who will be looking over your shoulder – parents, examination bodies, professional associations etc. And if you are teaching for an institution then they will certainly want to see some evidence of a teaching plan that reassures them that you know what you are doing.

Doing the subject justice

While I do not advocate a 'subject-centred' approach it is nonetheless important that you make sure that you cover the ground of your subject adequately. The fact that the students don't want to know about double entry book-keeping is no argument for restricting your accounts teaching to doing the petty cash book.

Yes, concentrate on what the students need to know, but also make sure that they are aware of the full range of the subject of study, particularly if that is the nature of your contract with them and/or with the college or in your advertising of the course. You would be failing in your duty as a professional freelance tutor if your students went away with a load of misconceptions about the subject or with great gaps in their awareness of what they had yet to learn.

Dealing with mixed abilities

You will hear professional teachers talking about 'mixed ability teaching' as if it were some kind of special teaching that you had to do once in a while, or as if it were some specialised branch of teaching.

Grasp the following concept and you will be several steps ahead of most teachers and tutors:

ALL TEACHING IS MIXED ABILITY TEACHING

You can immediately think of objections. If you start a beginners' group in your subject, one which most people will have no idea about before they begin, then surely that will not require mixed ability teaching? Believe me, it will. Why? Because **every human being is different and some people learn some things faster than others**. If I were in a learning group involving discussion and ideas I'm sure I'd get on well and get ahead of some of the other students. However, if I were in a class learning maths or book-keeping I know I would fall behind very rapidly.

In other words, as soon as you have progressed into the teaching a week or two, your students will begin to show differing abilities to grasp the subject and make progress – so you will, within a very short period, find yourself teaching a mixed ability group.

Remembering the range of teaching methods

Recognising the reality of the situation will help you to deal with mixed ability teaching and, as you will have learned in Chapter 3, the old-fashioned style of teaching involving lots of 'chalk and talk' is not flexible enough to deal with the variety of learning needs you will find within any group. Once you start using some of the other methods outlined in that chapter – discussion, individual and group work and so on – you will not even be aware of any difficulties from having a mixed ability group because these methods mean that you will be working with each individual's needs. What is more, you will find them easier and less stressful – and so will the students.

SETTING AIMS

Are your aims the same as the students' aims?

Setting aims and goals is an important starting point for learning and teaching. Bear in mind that your aims and goals may not be exactly the same as those of the students, so it is important to make the setting of aims and goals a two-way process.

Setting your overall or long-term goal

Working first with your own views and thoughts and then later with the input of the students, try to identify an overall aim for the course.

You might, for example, define it as 'becoming fully proficient in every aspect of pottery'. That might imply a course of lessons over five or six years on a part-time basis, so in one year you might identify the stages you could reasonably expect the students to reach. These might be:

- being able to prepare clay for use

- being able to use the basic building techniques such as moulds, coiling, making slab pots and throwing on the wheel

- being able to carry out basic decorating and glazing techniques

- ability to carry out firings for bisque and glazed ware with proper care and control of the kiln.

Identifying more immediate goals

These elements need to be broken down into subsidiary aims or goals which you can check the students' ability to carry out effectively. The various stages involved in achieving any of these goals need to be further broken down into more basic skills and goals. This process helps enormously in drawing up a course plan or syllabus.

DRAWING UP A FLEXIBLE COURSE OUTLINE

Before you even meet your group you will be starting to think of what it is that you will be teaching. Of course, you will take on board the principles of student-centred learning and try to imagine what your prospective students will want and need to learn.

Until you meet them, however, and possibly to satisfy the needs of the institution you may be teaching at, you will need to draw up a course outline. Make it clear, in a preamble, that this outline is flexible and will be adjusted to meet the needs of the students as the course progresses. You should then draw up, from your knowledge and experience, a list of topics or stages in your subject, putting them in a logical order from the new learner's perspective (see Figure 4).

Introducing the course

Your first session should be devoted to an introduction to the subject. That doesn't mean that you need to give a lecture: far better to start by making the students feel at home and asking them questions about what they know already about the subject, what they want to learn, why they are learning and what they hope to do with their learning. Your answers may well cover much of the ground of introducing the subject, but a short talk, preferably illustrated for interest, could follow this session so that the students get a rounded idea of what the subject encompasses.

A further session of questions could follow, this time with the students asking you questions on aspects they want to know more about. Invite them to write down questions, perhaps at a coffee break, as that will help those who are shy or afraid of showing up their ignorance.

NEGOTIATING WITH YOUR STUDENTS

The next stage is to go over with them the syllabus or course outline you have prepared and discuss it with them, stressing the flexibility of the plan and making sure that they express their learning needs.

6-week course: 'Writing for Beginners'

Week 1 Introducing self and students using interview techniques. Introduction to course: finding out areas students are interested in; assessing previous writing experience and/or previous publications; discussing aims of course and of individuals; practical writing exercise – share and discuss; looking at similar pieces by established writers – how do students pieces compare? Setting work to be done and brought to next meeting.

Week 2 Start by students reading out work and discussing constructively; describe and discuss some of the 'rules' of writing; why we write; consideration of audience; constraints of the marketplace; presentation on writing the feature article; dissecting three very different articles; set students to work out article outline and title; advise on an individual basis; question session; draw threads together; set writing of article for specific publication for next week.

Week 3 Pin articles on wall for all students to read and note comments; discuss and suggest improvements; identify possible markets and look up addresses to send them to; split class in two and give out short story to one group and poem to other; talk to poetry group about analysing poetry while other group reads story; poetry group work on analysing poem while other group discuss reactions to story with tutor; bring group together to discuss project to share their writing with college and/or community.

Week 4 Senior reporter from local paper to talk to group about writing for newspapers; question and discussion; students try their hand at writing up local story; talk about writing for radio; set radio script exercise; arrange visit to local radio station.

Week 5 Visit to local radio station – meet in foyer of station; talk and tour by presenter; group interview of students and tutor for programme.

Week 6 Review of radio visit and newspaper talk; marketing work to editors; resources for writing; becoming professional; how to lay out work; how to get work before you write it; writing a book proposal; further help and support with your writing; review of course.

Fig. 4. A sample course outline.

Getting them to write down their needs

Perhaps the best way is to formalise the earlier question and discussion sessions by asking them all to write down what, exactly, they want to gain from the course, what they want to learn and what they hope to do with their new learning.

From these slips of paper write down on the board the common topics or needs that come up so that everyone can see their own and everyone's needs coming together as the needs of the group as a whole. Ask for further ideas and clarification. Then go over your course outline with them, comparing it with the list on the board, and begin to modify it with them to produce a new course syllabus which reflects their learning needs at this point in time.

Ask them about the topics on your list that they have not identified as priorities. It may be that they have not thought about these areas or don't know enough to weigh their importance. Suggest that you review the new syllabus together in a few weeks' time and see if new needs emerge or they become aware of the need to study the areas you have identified but they do not consider a priority at the moment.

Offering other options

Remember that you are negotiating: the students are aware of their needs, you have a wider knowledge and understanding of the issues. While respecting their needs, you should not be afraid of suggesting other things you feel the students need to know.

Empowering your students

Negotiating is a very powerful and important process as it tells the students, right at the start, that they are involved in the learning process and have some control over their own learning. This is a very empowering concept which some will not be familiar with but which all will feel invigorating. It will set the tone for the rest of the course and raise the expectations they will have of themselves as partners in the learning process.

PLANNING AND RUNNING A LESSON

Using current issues

Like your course syllabus, your plans for individual lessons need to be reasonably flexible so that you can respond to needs that arise or take advantage of learning opportunities that present themselves which promise to be more profitable than what you had planned to do. You might, for example, if running a course on society or moral philosophy, pick up issues that arise from a particularly horrific murder case that everyone is talking about. Remember that people will learn from what interests them, not what they 'ought' to be interested in.

If your lesson planning is based on a variety of approaches you will have sections within your plan that can be dropped if necessary to accommodate other needs as they arise. If they are important, they can always be dealt with in a later lesson.

Planning your lesson in flexible units

Prepare your lesson in small units which are relatively self-contained. Try to estimate how much time they will take, always recognising that any single topic can expand to three times the length you estimate because the students either find it fascinating or difficult. Or you may find that what you thought would take twenty minutes or so is over in five minutes because the students find it boring or are unresponsive. It pays to have a few extra units in reserve to make sure that you always have enough material for a lesson.

Giving your lesson a logical structure

Think about the logical structure of the lesson. Perhaps you need some kind of introduction to the topic. You might give this in a five-minute talk or you could simply ask a range of questions which raise some of the topics, problems or issues which will lead you into the main content of the lesson.

A good formula to use in planning is **AIDA**, the salesman's friend. AIDA is a mnemonic to help salesmen to present a logically structured sales presentation:

- A for Attention

- I for Interest

- D for Desire (or Demonstration)

- A for Action

The steps are obvious once you think about them, but they are a helpful variation on the idea of having a beginning middle and end. If you can find some spectacular way of catching the group's **Attention** you will get their **Interest** and the **Desire** will grow to learn more through your **Demonstration** and they will go on to take **Action** by practising the skill themselves.

Having a clear plan

The important thing is to have some plan of what you want to happen in the lesson even if that plan is modified by interaction with the students (see Figure 5). Make sure you are clear about the aim of that particular session. What will you expect the students to have learned from it or be able to do at the end of it? Consider how it relates to the course as a whole. Give the students an overview of what the lesson will be about and make sure that the points learned are summarised in some way at the end.

Consider the proverbial advice given to new public speakers:

'Tell 'em what you're going to tell 'em; tell 'em it; then tell 'em what you've told 'em!'

Introduce self to group – ask them to make name badges – large so that we can all read them – ask to introduce themselves to us in a couple of sentences – ask to write down what they hope to gain from the course. (15 minutes)

Give overview of course and methods and approaches we will be using – ask for questions. (10 minutes)

Do the dream exercise – write down the big dream for their life if they could achieve anything they liked. Share and discuss implications both general and individual. (35–45 minutes)

COFFEE BREAK (15 minutes)

Talk about life goals and place of work/career in that perspective – cover aspects of self-confidence and positive thinking – questions and discussion. (20 minutes)

Discuss resources for course and course plan in the light of their expressed needs – ask what specific help they feel they need – prepare them for next week's skills analysis session. (20 minutes)

Fig. 5. A sample lesson plan (for the first meeting of a course on changing careers).

Repetition, **rehearsal** and **reinforcement** are important in the learning process. A useful pattern for this process is to begin by reviewing the previous lesson, assess the current state of the group's knowledge and pick up on the work you asked the students to do.

Throughout the lesson keep the interest level high by constantly assessing the level of comprehension, encouraging participation and getting the students to reflect back the main points. Conclude the session by reviewing the ground covered, testing the students' understanding and inviting questions.

Using notes and handouts

It helps if you can give out notes or summary sheets for students to take away, but don't hand them out during the lesson unless you are actually going to use them and work through them during the lesson, otherwise students will begin reading them and not pay attention to the lesson itself. Tell them you will be distributing notes so that they don't spend all their time trying to scribble down every word you say and not really understanding it.

How to plan

In planning for your lessons ask yourself the trigger questions **why**? **what**? **how**? **when**? **who**? **which**? and **where**? Plan the resources you will need to take, such as pictures, books, samples, tools etc. and arrange for any equipment you want to use such as a slide projector or video recorder. Think, too about the resources you want the students to bring – pens, notepads, materials and so on.

Writing it down

Some people do their lesson planning in their heads. That's fine, but don't leave it there. Pressures and distractions could mean that you forget much of what you had planned in your head, so you should always have a written plan to follow, however much of an outline sketch it is. Your lesson plan is your map of the learning journey you and your students are setting out on. It is your responsibility to have and to follow the map.

There is no 'right way'

Finally, no two people think or teach alike so there is no single perfect way to write a lesson plan. For some it may be just half a dozen key words on an index card, for others it could be several tightly written pages of notes. On the whole, somewhere between these two extremes seems the best place to start so that you are neither too casual nor too tied to a written script.

Setting up learning experiences

If you think of your lessons as workshops or laboratories of learning then you may find it easier to devise interesting ways of learning. Try to plan and set up learning experiences. These could be as simple as a list of four or five questions on a sheet which is given to the students in small groups to discuss; the provision of worn-out engine parts that students can take apart and reassemble; setting up an experiment; getting them to carry out a survey; or setting a puzzle or problem for them to solve. Remember: 'I **do** and I understand.'

CHECKING ON STUDENTS' ACHIEVEMENTS

Fundamental to your success as a freelance tutor or teacher is the ability to assess the success of the students' learning – and therefore of your teaching.

Assessment is usually linked in people's minds with exams, tests and formal recognition of their learning. It is, however, more important in its informal mode. Part of learning is confidence and that confidence comes from achievement. It is therefore vital that the students' achievements are measurable so that they can see that progress and gain confidence to go on and learn more.

Assessment is a co-operative enterprise

How do you assess students' progress? Try the following:

- Can you see that the student can do what you set out to teach him or her?

- Ask the students to demonstrate their new skills.

- Ask questions designed to show understanding of information or principles.

- Get the students to keep an assessment notebook or sheet in which they write their goals and note their achievements. This record can be reviewed by student and tutor together and used in planning future learning.

- Devise ways in which the students can demonstrate or 'show off' their achievement.

- Above all, if you and your students become goal and achievement oriented then learning and progress will take place.

MORE ON WORKING WITH GROUPS

Why people join groups

Individuals are drawn into groups for a variety of reasons which have nothing to do with learning. They may, for example, want to meet new friends, seek an outlet for their views, gain acceptance or seek self-importance. Being aware of these and other hidden motives may help you ensure that your group does not degenerate into a mere social group – you must keep control by exercising firm leadership.

It is you as the tutor who will set the tone and establish the values of the group right at the start by stressing the learning character of the group and setting a framework of values and principles within which the group will act.

Learning to be a leader

Leadership in groups is important with respect to learning. Research has shown that groups led by chairmen who are simply passive observers are unproductive, while those which are led by chairmen who exercise leadership are productive. Such leadership can come from the situation – as the tutor's does. It can be democratic, in the case of an elected leader, or authoritarian where the leadership is imposed. In any group there may be a challenge for the leadership of the group and strong characters may seek to usurp the tutor's leadership role. That is one of the reasons why it is important for the tutor to assert himself or herself at the beginning, laying down the expectations, procedures and format for the conduct of the learning and getting the group's tacit agreement on this.

Losing sight of the learning agenda

One of the biggest problems in learning groups is the private preoccupations of members of the group threatening to take over and replace the learning agenda. They will want to talk about their sick husband, boast about their fast cars or simply engage in incessant, irrelevant chatter. Why do they do it? And why do groups tolerate it? And what can the tutor do about it? Clearly, people expose these private aspects of their lives in class because it makes them important, focuses attention on them – and talking is enjoyable.

The group, on the other hand, tolerates this because it is seen as 'exciting' or 'different'. However, there will come a point when the group will indicate by hints, body language etc. that 'enough is enough – shut up and let's get on'. If this does not seem to be working on some insensitive members, you will find it easier than you think to suggest firmly that 'if we're not careful we'll be enjoying this chattering all night – let's get back to the lesson!'

THE STUDENTS' ROLE

Getting the students involved
This point has been made before, but it is worth stressing again that teaching and learning should be a fully collaborative venture. Part of the learning is in the sharing of responsibility and the growing sense of confidence and competence. So, if a class outing is suggested, let the students plan and organise it. All too often tutors let themselves become the slaves of the group they are teaching, rushing around arranging everything, carrying stuff around, shifting tables and chairs, and all the thousand and one other jobs that seem to crop up. Share them with the students and help the group to grow in ownership and organisation of the learning.

Making sure the students do the learning
Make it clear to your students that the responsibility for learning is theirs and that you are simply a resource to help them in that aim, using your leadership skills and sharing your knowledge and expertise with them. If they want to progress, then they will have to work. Help them, then, in the planning and teaching of your lessons to begin that process by making them work at the learning process in ways that they can take home with them and continue to work on.

Making your students independent
The aim of education is to draw out of the student the natural talent they have and to show them how to become independent. All your teaching should be devoted to that end. It is when your students do not need you any more that you know you have achieved success as a tutor.

CASE STUDIES

Linda learns from her students
When she first started teaching Linda was shown by the adult education centre principal how to draw up a syllabus or scheme of work. She tried to stick to this faithfully and found it frustrating when the

class got carried away in other directions. When she discussed this with the class they stressed what they had learned that wasn't on Linda's syllabus and she realised that she was being too rigid. She had discovered the need to negotiate learning with her students and realised that lesson plans were only a guide or a starting point on the learning journey.

Tom changes leadership style

As an ex-Marine sergeant, Tom had no difficulties with leadership of groups – or so he thought until he had a rebellion on his hands! At the end of a particularly difficult and gruelling weekend in which Tom had done a lot of shouting at his latest ''orrible lot', he noticed them in a huddle over dinner. After dinner at the final session of the course they all started to shout at him in unison, drowning out his protests. He got the message and has now modified his army style leadership for a quieter, more co-operative style.

Elaine and Eddie learn to be less formal

Having worked for so long within the school system and having to meet exam requirements exactly, Elaine and Eddie took a while to relax into more informal, but more effective methods. Realising the need for students to become more independent in their learning, they experimented with a range of self-administered worksheets and assessment tests which they use more widely in the group teaching they introduced to their tutorial agency. This gives students more control over the pace of their learning and they are more motivated and independent. What is more, it makes the tutor's role more that of a consultant, able to help with learning difficulties more effectively.

Tim cracks the problem and slashes the cost of his courses

Much of the expense of a correspondence or home study course of the kind that Tim provides is in the time it takes for tutors to mark and assess student assignments. Having created a carefully structured course in photography himself he put his mind to the problem and devised a system of self-administered tests and assessments that come with his courses. This meant that he could slash the cost of the courses, while difficulties and queries that his students still have are submitted on a special sheet which the student sends in with a small fee.

CHECKLIST

1. Who is your 'hidden' customer? Parent? College? Exam or professional body? What kind of course outline do you need to prepare to satisfy them?

2. Do you need to produce something a bit more 'user friendly' for the students? What should it cover? Draw up a course outline for an appropriate number of weeks.

3. Write down what you think the students will be looking for in specific detail. What will be their fears and difficulties?

4. Draw up a list of questions you can ask the students in order to find out their learning needs in your subject.

5. Can you write down, in one sentence the overall aim of your course? Can you define that in behavioural terms (i.e. what the students will be able to *do* at the end of it)?

6. Can you write down a specific aim or goal for each of the teaching sessions you have outlined in your course syllabus (see 2 above)? If not you need to rethink that session.

7. Draft a list of teaching units you could put together for use in your lessons.

8. Write a list of the resources available to you for incorporation into your lessons.

9. Think about (and write down) any concrete ways you can think of to assess students' progress in any aspect of what you will be teaching in your course.

5
Getting Work in Schools and Colleges

In this chapter we will have a look at the educational system and how it works, as well as how you, as a freelance teacher and tutor, can get in.

THE SYSTEM AND HOW IT WORKS

The local authority system
When we talk about 'the system' we are referring to the publicly provided system of education from nursery and primary schools up to and including the universities, but not including private schools (called, in some quaint twist of British logic, 'public' schools!) and other educational enterprises run for commercial gain (or sometimes as charities).

Until fairly recently the public education system was easy to describe, as there was a relative uniformity of organisation and administration across the country. This common structure is crumbling now, with education being forced to follow the trend of privatisation and deregulation from its old masters, the county or metropolitan councils (local education authorities or LEAs) which invariably delegated much local control to an area education office of some kind. Where such structures remain, their function is curtailed and schools and colleges are being encouraged, if not forced, to become independent and responsible for the control of their own budgets and other affairs.

For the aspiring freelance tutor or teacher this has both plus points and minus points. While the central administration was once a source of direct employment where one could at least register an interest and be appointed to various panels or registers for tutoring or part-time or occasional teaching, it is more likely to be the case now that you will have to apply directly to the educational establishment itself. While this means more effort contacting a larger number of possible employers, it does at least mean more of a free market where, if your face does not fit in one place, it may well be eagerly welcomed in another.

Types of educational provision
These places can be categorised as being one of the following:

- Nursery schools.

- Primary schools.

- Junior schools.

- Middle schools.

- Secondary schools (which may be comprehensive, single sex, technical, grammar or other specialist type).

- Sixth form colleges (which may cover further education functions, including adult education).

- Further education (post-16 vocational education, but can also include the same academic work as sixth form colleges).

- Special education (covering a wide range of provision including schools for the mentally subnormal, the deaf, school refusers, provision for autistic children and young adults etc.).

- Higher education (universities and higher level colleges, most traditionally independent of local authority control). Don't forget that most universities have large extra-mural or adult education departments which rely on large numbers of part-time specialist tutors. This is also very largely true of art colleges and some other specialist higher education establishments.

- Adult education (classes in largely non-vocational subjects for recreation and self-development).

Looking at provision in your area
The pattern of provision has always varied from area to area and the deregulation which has occurred in recent years has made the situation even more fragmented.

What you will need to do is to look at the pattern of provision in your own area – a survey of the market, if you like. To begin this, start by approaching the local education authority either at a local, area office if there is one, or at the town or county hall.

Ask if they have any information about schools and other educational establishments in your area, explaining that you are interested in some teaching or tutoring. Ask for their advice and any help they can give you.

Reconnoitre the neighbourhood (defining this as how far you are prepared to travel for work) and identify schools, colleges and other educational units around. Use the local phone book or *Yellow Pages* to make lists of those within the distance range you are happy to work within. Don't eliminate any of these at the start, as you may be surprised at the range of subjects studied and the opportunities there may be in the unlikeliest of places.

MAKING YOUR APPROACH

Deciding who to approach
Unless there are obvious choices for you based on your own knowledge of the area and the skills you have to offer, the short answer is that you ought to approach every possible user of your services – after all, there will be relatively few schools, colleges and other establishments within your area.

Deciding how to approach
You may decide that a telephone approach is best. However, most sales people don't recommend relying on a single medium of approach to any market.

A good strategy, therefore, is to make use of several approaches in a concerted campaign that is more likely to get results. One such approach would be to write a brief introductory letter seeking to raise interest in seeing you and following this up by a brief telephone call.

WRITING WINNING LETTERS

Your aim in an initial letter is to get an informal interview, for it is most unlikely that there will be work just waiting for someone like you to write in. It is much easier in an informal chat to explore all the possibilities there may be for someone like you in an establishment. A letter offering to teach drama, for example, is likely to lead to a direct 'no' with no mention of the fact that someone is needed for music, which you may also be able to offer. This is much more likely to come up in an informal discussion and lead to an offer of some work.

Getting an interview
The secret of getting interviews which may lead to work is very simple – and not many people will know it, which will give you a great advantage. It is this: don't write asking if there is any work for you. Instead, write asking if the head would be willing to spare a little of his or her time to give you some advice on breaking into part-time teaching or tutoring. (See Figure 6.)

14 Hopeful Crescent
Anytown
Hopeshire
OK1 2IT

Tel: (01010) 111222

2 October 199X

Mr Tom Head
Headmaster
Anytown Comprehensive
Academy Street
Anytown
AC2 3UP

Dear Mr Head

I am writing to you in the hope that you can help me with some advice about taking up part-time teaching or tutoring now that my family are of an age that allows me to consider the possibility of returning to work in a limited way.

I understand that as head of a large school your time is heavily committed, but I would very much appreciate it if you would be prepared to spare fifteen minutes of your valuable time to give me the benefit of your experience and expertise to advise on how to approach the business of becoming a part-time tutor.

A copy of my CV is enclosed to give you some idea of my background before we meet.

Any day of the week would be convenient for me to come and see you at a time suitable to you. I hope that you will feel able to fit me into your busy schedule.

I look forward to hearing from you.

Yours sincerely

(Mrs) A. Hopeful

Fig. 6. Sample letter to a local school head.

People hate to be asked for work, because it puts them in the awkward position of probably having to say 'no', but they *love* to be asked for advice! On this basis, you are likely to get an appointment for a short discussion where the important man or woman will give you valuable advice – and *may* just offer you a job as well!

BUT – and this is important – **you must never ask directly for work**. Listen to the advice given. Find out all you can about the opportunities, the demands, the problems, the approach. And *always* ask towards the end of the allocated time if he or she knows of anyone else you could approach for further advice. Why?

The reason is simple. He or she may well know of a colleague who needs someone like you. They may call them up while you are there and arrange for you to see this person. Or they may talk to a colleague later who is bemoaning the lack of good drama teachers and the person who interviewed you may say, 'I just happen to have been talking to someone last week – I think I've still got their number in my diary . . .' and a job is offered to you out of the blue. This is the technique known as **networking** and it is very effective – it is reckoned by some that 75–80 per cent of jobs are filled in this way without advertising.

Your letter must be typed on a crisp, white sheet of A4 paper using a good electric typewriter or word processor: the impression you want to give is of someone who is fully professional.

USING THE TELEPHONE TO GET INFORMATION AND APPOINTMENTS

You can use the telephone in two ways: to replace the approach by letter outlined above, or to follow up the letter within 4–7 days of sending it.

The difficulty in using the telephone as your first approach is that it may be the last – and briefest – chance you get! It will be difficult to get through to the head in the first place as he or she will be a busy executive with meetings, letters and reports to deal with – overworked as most executives are. The head's secretary will try to put you off and even if you should manage to get through you may well be fobbed off with two minutes worth of off-the-cuff advice which will not serve your purpose.

Far better to write as suggested and then use the telephone to reinforce the message. Call and ask to speak to them by name. If asked by the receptionist what it is about simply say that it is about your correspondence with the head (naming them). This may well get you through the protective barrier. Once through, you should say something like:

> 'Mr Head, my name is Ann Hopeful and I'm just ringing to make sure you received my letter. I wrote asking if you would be good enough to see me to give me some advice about a possible career in teaching and tutoring. Is it possible for you to spare me fifteen minutes some time?'

Focus on getting an appointment – try not to let them discuss your request over the phone.

PUTTING TOGETHER A RELEVANT CV

The purpose of a CV is to summarise, in an easily readable form, your work and life experience, presenting it in such a way as to make you seem ideal for the job you are applying for.

This means that you need to have it in some flexible form, ideally on computer, so that you can adjust it to emphasise the most relevant facts for each job application.

Of course, if you are making a speculative approach, such as is suggested in this chapter, you can't do this very accurately. However, you can think about the particular school or college you are approaching and try to assess, from what you know of it, how to present yourself in a way which will fit their needs as far as you can estimate them.

Make your CV a 'dynamic' CV. Don't clutter up the beginning with too much information about yourself and irrelevant early detail. Start with your name and address and barest facts, such as date of birth.

Follow this with a summary, in about 25–75 words, of what you are in professional terms and what you have, broadly, to offer. (Three examples are given in Figure 7.) This gives the person reading the CV an immediate summary of what is on offer and he or she can then look further for more detailed information about education, work experience and so on, which should follow.

Try to keep your dynamic CV to a single, clearly typed page. Give less detail about early schooling and experience and most detail about later education. Do the same for work experience except where particular earlier experience is more relevant.

In everything you write show what you have **achieved**, not just what you **did** a job. Show what you can **do** for the prospective employer.

Compare the following two extracts:

ANN HOPEFUL: a trained drama teacher (Rose Bruford College) with 12 years experience teaching in schools and colleges (1963–75). Worked regularly with Anytown Amateur Dramatic Society producing and directing and taught occasional weekend courses for Youth Service and Women's Institute. Strong musical background (piano and guitar). Now looking for part-time or occasional work teaching drama and or music to secondary level and beyond.

DARREN WEBB: Wood turner and sculptor (self-taught). Earned full-time living from studio work since 1992. Exhibited in many arts and craft shows and work is in a number of private and public collections. Have run short courses for adults in own studio and taught for Faraway County Council on summer schools and have done some basic tutor training in the teaching of adults. Interested in teaching sculpture. wood carving or wood turning to adult education classes.

JENNY POLDI: I was born in Italy of Anglo-Italian parents in 1955 but have lived in this country for the last twenty years. I run a small Italian-style restaurant and am interested in teaching Italian in schools or colleges and in teaching adult education classes in Italian Cookery.

Fig. 7. Examples of personal summary for CV.

1. 'I taught drama for two years at Nextown High School and also did some music teaching to the sixth form (piano and guitar).'

2. 'At the end of two years teaching a drama course at Nextown High School, four of my thirteen students were awarded places in Drama school (two at RADA) and through the coaching I gave two students went from the sixth form to the Royal Academy of Music on scholarships.'

You see the difference? The first is just saying 'I was there, I passed the time teaching' while the second is focused on results. It is the results which count and the results which will sell you to a potential employer.

Don't elaborate too much in your CV. If you need to say something about your general availability or expand on any aspect of the brief facts in your CV you should do this in a short, accompanying letter (again, no longer than a single-sided sheet of neatly typed paper).

Oh, and don't, whatever you do, try to attract attention to yourself by having your CV on dayglo paper or in a complicated folder like some fancy piece of artwork or design. Keep it plain, smart and businesslike. Stand out by the quality of the offer you make. Make yourself and what you offer so irresistibly relevant that the person reading will *have* to see you!

PRESENTING YOURSELF AT INTERVIEW

There are a number of things to remember about interviews:

- The first is that it is **a two-way process**. You are there as much to make up your mind about whether you would like to work in this place with these people, as for them to make the decision about whether they want you to work for them. Remember this and it will take the edge off any nervousness you may feel.

- **First impressions** are important and virtually ineradicable, so:
  - be on time
  - be smart and appropriately dressed
  - smile!

- **Don't regard questions as 'tricks'**. Good interviews depend on an honest and open exchange of information and views. Don't feel you have to agree with everything your interviewer says, but be tactful.

- **If asked for your views give them straightforwardly**. Don't worry about not getting the job – there is nothing worse than getting a job in a place where you don't fit and there's nothing less convincing than an answer that goes, 'On the one hand . . . but on the other hand . . .'.

- If you want to impress the interviewer remember what was stressed above about CVs – **demonstrate your achievements**. Take along the certificate you were awarded for the Best Producer in the Amateur Drama Festival; show a sparkling photograph of one of your stunning stage sets; hand over a menu from your Italian restaurant; put one of your relief carvings on the desk; throw off a few attractive sounding Italian phrases. In short, show them what you can do – *for them.*

- **Be positive.** Talk about how you will teach your class, how you could use the stage in the hall, when and where you could plan an exhibition of students' work, how your cookery students will get behind the scenes at your restaurant, what your music or drama group will contribute to the Christmas show and so on.

- Go to the interview armed with ideas, with course outlines, with strategies for promoting your course, with questions about what you will be allowed to do to expand and develop the subject. **Be interested.**

- **Finally, be direct.** Towards the conclusion of the interview ask for the job (assuming that your interview is not one you have arranged for advice only):

> 'Well, Mr Head, what do you think? Could you use a course on Italian Cookery?'

or

> 'What about it Mr Head, would you like to try out a short one-term course on wood carving as a start?"

or

> 'Mr Head, in ten weeks I could have your students putting on a show for parents at Christmas. What do you think?"

GETTING YOUR FOOT IN THE DOOR

Just supposing your Mr Head isn't moved to action by your offer or is humming and hawing. What do you do? Make him an offer he can't refuse. Offer him a free trial:

> 'Mr Head, I know it's difficult for you – what if I were to offer to do a one-day Drama Workshop for you in the summer term, completely free? Then if there's enough interest and you're pleased with the way it goes, we could talk about a longer course for the following term.'

Could you resist an offer like that? I know I couldn't unless there was some overriding reason why I simply wouldn't, couldn't have you near my educational establishment – like you're a known child molester or you have a huge personal hygiene problem.

Go for it!

CASE STUDIES

Linda serves a cream tea

When Linda wanted to extend her jam-making classes to a nearby town's adult education centre, she sent a miniature pot of her jam to the tutor in charge with a card which said, 'Please don't open until I bring the scones! Give me a ring on Anytown 121212.' Intrigued, the tutor rang Linda and Linda arranged to pop in that afternoon to, as she said, 'put forward a proposition'. She duly arrived, opened her bag, took out a couple of scones and spread them with some butter and the jam from the miniature pot and talked about her jam-making classes. As you might imagine, she got the extra work!

Tim capitalises on his skills

Being a writer and publisher of correspondence courses you'd think that Tim would be good at writing letters – and you'd be right! Tim used his copywriting skills to approach a number of adult education principals with a sales letter which offered to help them out with groups of students which were too small to form classes in a number of subjects. He offered a deal in which he would provide study material in a distance learning package for half the cost of the student fees. This meant that the adult centre kept half the fees that they would have had to refund anyway and Tim got the other half. Since he had no marketing costs, this represented profitable business for him and the students got their courses. A good deal all round.

CHECKLIST

1. Get to know the structure and range of educational establishments in your area.

2. Contact the county or town hall and the local area office of your local education authority and find out what establishments there are and what they can tell you about teaching and tutoring opportunities.

3. Draft a dynamic CV for use in your work-seeking campaign.

4. Write to potential employers in schools and colleges with a request for an interview for advice about taking up tutoring and teaching.

5. Follow up with a phone call to press for an interview.

6. Whether in CV, letter or interview stress your achievements in terms of the results you can also get for the potential employer.

7. Try to make a good first impression at interview and remember that you are interviewing them as well.

8. If there seems little chance of paid tutoring, offer to do a little free teaching with no obligation – get your foot in the door.

6
Selling to the Commercial Sector

Much of what was covered in Chapter 5 applies also to the business of getting work as a freelance teacher or tutor in the commercial sector, so this will be one of the shortest chapters in the book!

Clearly, while the same principles apply to seeking and applying for available work in this sector, there will be considerable differences in emphasis both from the state sector and between the widely differing organisations in the commercial field.

The commercial field is much more varied than the LEA sector of education, taking in as it does a whole host of small, independent providers, large commercial tutoring organisations and the whole field of training both by specialist training firms and within businesses themselves.

IDENTIFYING THE APPROPRIATE OPPORTUNITIES

With the increasing privatisation of education throughout the range, there is a growth in small organisations or businesses offering tuition in specialist areas. These will include clubs and societies, where teaching is often of a voluntary nature, as well as agencies set up as profit-making businesses like computer schools, dancing academies or fitness studios.

LOOKING FOR OTHER LEARNING ORGANISATIONS

The local press
Apart from your general knowledge and awareness of local provision, much of the commercial provision can be found from two or three sources. The most obvious of these is the advertising pages of the local paper, for, as commercial operations, they depend on attracting clients by advertising their services just like any other business.

Yellow Pages
In addition, time spent trawling *Yellow Pages* under Educational Ser-

vices, Educational Holiday Organisers, Tutoring, Training Services and
specific subject-related headings like Secretarial Training, Word Processing Services, Music Teachers and the more generic Schools and
Colleges should turn up a wealth of opportunity for you to explore.

The reference library
Don't forget to do some research at the library where the research
librarian will prove a gold mine of information and advice in your
quest.

YOUR APPROACH

Approaching your chosen targets in the commercial sector will be
essentially no different from the approach recommended in the previous chapter, although you will find some differences in attitude.

Varying standards
Remember that first and foremost, these organisations are businesses
and exist in order to make a profit at the end of the day. You will
find that standards and expectations will vary enormously, with some
being very professional and demanding, while others will be more
easy-going and less concerned with academic excellence, preferring
solid hands-on experience in those who apply for work with them.
Try to find out what approach they take before applying to them and
tailor your approach accordingly.

Market oriented
As with any commercial enterprise, they will be more attuned to the
concept of marketing and will be more likely to appreciate your
focusing on customer satisfaction as the goal of your teaching. Some
will be more interested in technical competence, while others will welcome your thoughtful educational approach.

Selling the learning concept
You may well find that the principles you have learned from reading
this book will go down well when you explain the approach to teaching and learning that you would bring to their clients. Remember to
sell yourself and your approach in terms of their needs – that customers need to be satisfied and will be satisfied because you will meet
their learning needs and keep them coming back for more. You have
to show them that by taking you on they stand to profit more than
you stand to gain.

THE RATE FOR THE JOB

If teaching rates fluctuate wildly, they will do so more in the commercial sector where you will find rates offered at the bottom of the survival scale (often with organisations running government sponsored training for the unemployed) to unbelievably high daily rates for high powered management courses where the average rate will be around £250–£500 a day.

Be willing to negotiate and, if you feel the need in order to get a foothold, make them an offer they can't refuse. Suggest either a 'no-satisfaction, no fee' deal or a sample course free or for expenses only as a test run – it's a win-win situation they are unlikely to refuse.

TRAINING PAYS

You might decide, depending on what skills you have to offer, to go for the highest returns by trying to break into the training market where just two or three days work a month could bring you in all the income you need – three days at £500 a day every month would provide you with an income equal to the national average at around £18,000 a year – for part-time work!

Of course, you would have to spend a fair bit of time and some pretty tough selling to get the work, but it would be worthwhile in the long term. Bear in mind, however, that it is a crowded market with a large number of very professional firms competing for the business. It's hard for a single individual without a track record to get a foot in the door.

RESIDENTIAL EDUCATION

One way into this more lucrative marketplace is to approach the residential colleges offering a weekend or three-day course in your subject. That way, the college takes on the job of promoting and marketing the course and your reputation would be enhanced when you offer the same course directly to industry and business.

SEMINARS AND ONE-DAY WORKSHOPS

Offering a limited 'taster' in your subject is an appealing option for commercial and non-commercial providers alike. It does not commit them to great expenditure and enables them to test-run both you and the subject on offer, besides making an attractive and varied offering in their programme.

Ultimately the setting up of your own teaching and training business offers the greatest possibilities for exploiting your subject and your skills, placing them and how they are marketed under your direct control. This is what we move on to consider in the next chapter.

CHECKLIST

1. Research your area thoroughly to find out what commercially run educational providers exist.

2. Tailor your approach to the ethos of the individual commercial organisations you choose to approach.

3. Sell prospective commercial employers your understanding of good learning techniques as well as your subject competence – it's an area they are very often not strong on themselves.

4. Target the training market (if appropriate) as the best paying section of the commercial market.

5. Offer your services to residential colleges, private or public.

6. Offer seminars and one-day courses as 'tasters'.

7
Setting Up Your Own Independent Enterprise

Given the trend already identified of an increasingly fragmented and privatised educational provision, there are more and more opportunities to exploit the market for independent learning opportunities – particularly in niche markets.

As I write I read in my local paper not only of the local education authority's adult education classes, but of educational evenings laid on by the new Tate Gallery in St Ives, a Penzance gallery offering a ten-week winter art school and a new private school of music to open in St Ives next year with tuition in piano, violin, guitar, organ, recorder, singing etc. for both adults and children. Within the advertisement announcing this development is an expression of interest in hearing from 'teachers of other disciplines such as woodwind, brass, strings, early music, speech and drama'. For a considerable number of years my wife and I ran, from our home in Cornwall, a series of very successful residential 'Escape Weeks' – career change workshops for teachers wishing to get out of teaching.

The demand is there for all sorts of learning – all it needs is for some enterprising person to tap into the learning needs of people in the community.

FINDING YOUR NICHE

Looking at what is available

The key to successful marketing of any business or service these days is in finding a niche – a gap in the market that isn't already covered. Just look at your local newsagent's shelves: you will find scores of titles devoted to the most specific and obscure interests and pursuits, with very few general interest titles. It is part of the general fragmentation of the world that we see in every sphere and is partially the result of the enormous growth of knowledge and information that can lead to 'information overload'. Because we can't take in or cope with everything that is out there competing for our attention, we focus on a few single, narrow interests with which we can cope and retreat into them.

Use that trend and find your own niche market as a freelance teacher and tutor.

What can you offer?

Start with the range of skills and knowledge you have at your disposal (have another look at Chapter 2) to see how you can capitalise on this narrow focus that the world takes. Remember to play around with your knowledge and experience so that it is as adaptable as possible. Your skills in the martial arts, for example, would probably be of more interest presented as 'Keeping Killers at Bay' or 'Make Mugs of the Muggers!' rather than as pure courses in Kendo or Kung Fu.

What gaps are there in the market?

Do an extensive survey of what already exists in your locality in terms of local authority evening classes, private schools and classes, clubs and associations and so on. What isn't on offer? What needs can you identify that no one else is covering? Can you create a new interest for people to take up? Can you put a new slant on what is already being offered or offer it to a new clientele? Could you offer 'Computers for Grandparents', for example, or 'Six Magic Words that Will Increase Any Shop's Sales'. (Those six words could be, 'Come in and try one free' – and the course could go on to look at copywriting and/or simple marketing techniques to improve trade.)

Being opportunistic

Successful freelance teachers and tutors are reactive as well as proactive. It's fine to go out actively trying to create a new demand as suggested in the above section, but be alert to the opportunities that come your way, such as a newspaper report that indicates a learning need. Perhaps there's a newspaper item about the local college closing a popular course or transferring some activities to a site further away as a process of rationalisation. This is your chance to jump in and take up the slack by offering to provide what is being taken away. Perhaps it is a teacher or tutor who is moving away or who has died, creating a space for your services – if you react to it in a positive way.

GOING IT ALONE

You are in control

One of the nice things about running your own learning and teaching enterprise is that you are totally in control. You can set your own targets, make your own decisions about the best way to recruit and teach students, decide who you are going to target as your market and what you will offer them.

At the same time, these same positive elements have their negative aspects. Some people may find the idea of having to run their own enterprise, being their own marketing manager, administrative officer, accounts clerk, post boy, advertising copywriter and secretary, as well as teaching, somewhat daunting. If that is the way you feel, then running your own educational enterprise is not for you.

For others, however, it is the only way. To be in charge of your own destiny, making your own decisions by which you profit – or lose – is the most satisfying thing in the world. And it can be extremely profitable, with inbuilt advantages in terms of tax-deductible expenses and other benefits such as being able to choose your own working hours within the constraints of the needs of the business and choosing your working partners rather than having to work with people with whom you have little in common. Who knows, your fledgling teaching enterprise could end up as a chain of nationwide tutorial agencies or a large and profitable correspondence college.

Figure 8 sets out some of the basic facts and guidelines you need to be aware of when setting up your own business.

HOW BIG IS YOUR AMBITION?

Some of the decisions you will have to make will be determined by the vision you have of your business enterprise. Will it begin in a small, part-time way and remain such, or will it grow from these beginnings to a larger, more ambitious and impressive affair?

To help you form some idea of where you might be heading with your business before it begins, try writing down an idealised description of your business as you would like it to be in, say, ten years time. Your ideal might read something like this:

Beginning in a spare room in my house, I will begin teaching a creative writing class to a small group of 6–10 people. Once that group is established I will then add a course in commercial writing, including copywriting and further courses in writing novels, non-fiction books and feature writing for magazines. Once the business grows I will look for suitable office premises in town and re-launch the business as the Word-Power School of Writing with a long-term plan of franchising the concept in half-a-dozen other major towns to begin with.

- You can trade under your own name (**sole trader**) – simplest and best.

- You can set up a **partnership** with your spouse or a friend – but you will be legally responsible for the decisions and debts of your partner(s). Always have a legal agreement drawn up.

- You can be a **limited company** with an 'off-the-shelf' name or one you choose yourself. A company is a separate entity in law and you are not personally responsible for its debts unless you have acted illegally as a director.

- Open a **separate bank account** for your business. If you are not using a business name it is cheaper simply to open a second personal account discreetly.

- You will need some **stationery** – mainly letterheads and cards. Invoices etc. can simply be typed on a letterhead.

- Get an **accountant** – an exploratory interview should be free. Invariably an accountant will save you more than his or her fees.

- Your accountant will help you set up a simple and efficient way of keeping the **financial records** you will need for tax purposes – as well as for your own monitoring of the business. Early losses can be set against tax liabilities from other earnings.

- You will only have to **register for VAT** when your takings reach the registration limit – £47,000 at the time of writing. Keep good records of VAT paid as you can claim back VAT paid on goods and equipment (and services in some circumstances) bought before registration.

Fig. 8. Basics of business.

This long-term view will begin to shape the details of your business. What kind of image do you want to project? What kind of clients do you want to attract? What age groups are you targetting? Will it be up-market, or cheap and cheerful? What price structure will you adopt?

DECIDING ON PREMISES

The argument against **renting** premises is that it is a huge expense (together with business rates, heating, lighting, furnishing and so on) which has to be paid for before you can draw a penny out of the business for yourself. On the other hand, it gives your business a much more professional image and a high visibility in the marketplace. Many people will feel more comfortable about attending a school with its own premises than entering someone's front room for lessons.

To a large extent the decision will depend not only on your vision of the kind of business you want to build but on the amount of capital you have to launch your enterprise. For most people it is likely to be a compromise of starting from a home base or from casually hired premises and going on from there as the business becomes more successful.

CREATING AN IMAGE

Whether you start in a modest home-based way or in a more substantial way, the question of image is important. You may prefer to be seen simply as an individual personal tutor operating a homely and friendly service, or your ambitions may be greater.

Good design in your stationery and other literature will help to create that image and it is well worth paying for some professional design and a professionally developed logo that identifies your business. Try approaching the local art school, where you may find a student to do you a design for a very reasonable cost, or the Graphic Design department might like to take on your commission as an exercise for which you will make a small award to the winning student.

Your teaching material – notes, booklets etc. – should also be part of that designed image and produced as professionally as possible. Think of it as laying the foundations for your larger empire in the future where these materials will be used in half a dozen flourishing and well-regarded centres. It is all investment in the future.

RECORD-KEEPING

Do some careful thinking about the kinds of records you will need to keep:

- records of students and their progress,
- records of potential students who enquire, so that you can mail them on a regular basis until they become paying clients
- records of potential and actual tutors
- records of resources
- not forgetting the financial records you will need to monitor the progress of your business and to meet your tax liabilities.

Do not forget, by the way, to put aside money from your takings to pay your tax bills – failure to do so being one of the biggest causes of business failure in small one-person businesses.

PRICING YOUR SERVICES

To some extent you will be able to set your prices from your knowledge of charges made by other teaching organisations in your locality. You may decide to pitch your prices a bit lower than your competitors in the hope of attracting more students by undercutting them.

Calculating your desired income

A far better policy is to work out what you need to charge bearing in mind both your expenses and your desired level of income. An important part of that equation is to allow both for holidays and for the time you will be spending doing the 'non-productive' yet necessary work of the accounts, letter writing, tax and other form filling, visiting the bank manager and accountant etc.

Once you have deducted the time taken up by those activities you will be left with a realistic number of 'earning hours'. Deduct 15–20 per cent from that figure to allow for cancellations and unfilled slots, then use the number of hours left to divide into the weekly amount you want to earn, say, £250 a week divided by 25 hours tutoring – that is £10 an hour.

Don't simply settle for that figure as your rate, but add at least 20–30 per cent to cover expenses and running costs and a further 20–30 per cent to provide an overall profit for business growth, replacement of equipment etc. and profitability. That gives you a rate of £14.40–£16.90 per hour, so for a course of 10 one-and-a-half-hour lessons you should be charging a minimum of £216.

Fees for small group tuition

To be more productive, you can cut the cost to your students by offering small group tuition, so that with a group of 3–5 people paying, say, £8 an hour (£120 for 10 lessons of one-and-a-half hours) you would be grossing between £24 and £40 an hour or £360–£600 from that tutoring slot over 10 weeks. With 14 such sessions a week you would be bringing £5,040–£8,400 into the business over a ten-week period and perhaps a gross annual income for the business of £20,160–£33,600.

Paying others to do the teaching

Of course there is a limit to the actual teaching you can do by yourself and once you bring in other people to do some, if not all of the teaching, paying them, say, £12 an hour, each ten-week group would show a gross profit after wages of £180–£420. Theoretically there is no limit to the number of groups you could be running.

In the next chapter we will be considering the many ways in which you can set up a wealth-creating business in teaching and tutoring and related activities.

CASE STUDIES

Linda settles for part-time work

Linda's teaching and tutoring business is a good example of a business that started at home with jam-making and branched out to teaching adult education classes. Linda is content simply to teach half a dozen classes from which she earns a good part-time income of around £4,000. She has no premises or equipment to worry about and no administration to speak of, as she is paid on PAYE by the local authority.

The sergeant's in charge!

Tom went straight into a fully fledged educational business in a substantial way by selling his house and combining it with his army gratuity and his savings. He had the advantages of administration and other relevant experience to apply to the running of a business and was able to see how the skills he gained in the Royal Marines could be adapted to fill a niche in 'outward bound' type management training.

Premises of his own were essential to this type of business and fortunately they could also provide him both with his home and with other earning potential in between courses.

As a strong-minded character he likes the aspect of being totally in charge of his own show and is very happy making a good living from his establishment, with no ambitions beyond continuing to enjoy his present level of success.

Elaine and Eddie's business continues to expand

Eddie and Elaine started their tutorial business in the front room of their home on a part-time basis, supplementing their income by supply teaching. The addition of their multi-level-marketing business in health supplements could also be run from a home base, but when their tutorial agency began to expand by taking on other tutors they moved to a small suite of offices in the local town centre, giving them a much more professional image and a higher profile in the marketplace. After three years they are now looking for larger premises as their business continues to expand.

CHECKLIST

1. Think carefully before deciding to follow the self-employment route: have you the right kind of personality to cope with the demands?

2. Have you a unique offering to sell in the educational marketplace? Have you looked at what is already available in your area? Is there a niche market that is not being provided for?

3. Consider what training you may need to undertake to run your own business successfully. This may simply be reading some books on setting up your own business.

4. Make sure that you find yourself some good professional advisers, particularly a good accountant and a helpful bank manager. Find out what free business advice is available through your local Training and Enterprise Council and other sources.

5. Set down in writing a vision of your business as you think it could become. This will help you to be clear about whether or not you should be looking for premises and help you to formulate a sensible and realistic business plan.

6. Before you begin, give a lot of careful thought to how you will organise and administer the business. What records will you need and what is the best way to keep them? What image do you want your business to have?

7. Spend plenty of time working out the financial side of your business. What expenses will be incurred? (Overestimate rather than underestimate these.) What will you charge for your services? (Don't make the mistake of undercharging: ask yourself how much the market will bear.) How much business will you generate? (Underestimate rather than overestimate this.)

8
Ideas and Projects

This chapter provides a quick run-through of ideas and projects on which you could build a profitable learning business. It is intended as an ideas stimulator and does not attempt to outline how these particular ideas and projects could be set up – entrepreneurs are expected to do some of their own thinking! Not all of the ideas are directly concerned with freelance teaching and tutoring – some are in associated fields. Hopefully, the ideas in this section will spark off other ideas which may be more suitable or more profitable for you.

Private tuition
This is the obvious starting point for profiting from your skills. Remember your earnings will be limited by the number of actual hours you can work. Think either of expanding to the next project or of teaching in small groups to increase your hourly rate.

Running a tutorial agency
To the old saw, 'Those who can, do; those who can't, teach' could be added the entrepreneurial teacher's wisdom, 'Those who organise others to teach, make money'! Or, as John Paul Getty is reputed to have said, 'I would rather have 1 per cent of 100 men's efforts than 100 per cent of my own efforts.'

Supply teaching
While supply teaching might be thought of as only offering earning possibilities for trained teachers, with the process of devolvement of budgets to schools under increasing privatisation, there is an opportunity for the setting up of private agencies to supply this need that schools have.

Schools instructor
As we have made clear earlier in the book, not being a trained teacher may not be a barrier to working in schools as an instructor

at lower (but still good) rates of pay. As in the above project, there must also be potential in running an agency for schools instructors.

Independent schools
While traditional private schools are finding times hard in the current financial climate, there is nevertheless an increasing demand for both smaller schools and schools upholding a particular ethos, and opportunities abound for setting up, perhaps with other teachers, small day schools to meet this need.

Job clubs
Whatever form the various government schemes to help the unemployed take, there will always be scope for job clubs and career change workshops to help people into employment or to change career direction.

Computer-based learning
This is the wave of the future and computer learning is going to be a highly significant medium of education. Opportunities which suggest themselves range from running computer-based clubs and workshops in a variety of subjects (including computer literacy) to writing and devising educational programmes for computer-based learning.

Leisure learning
This encompasses a vast field and it is one which is wide open to private enterprise as adult education is forced to become more and more self-supporting financially, thus making it easier to compete with local authority provision – particularly in popular areas like keep fit and yoga where numbers could allow for keen pricing against standard adult education fee structures. (They can't cut the fees because they need the larger numbers to subsidise, say, third year Russian classes.)

Nursery school
Nursery education is seen as a growing priority and it is doubtful whether local authority provision will ever soak up the need in this area.

Learning holidays
This is a huge growth area from which you can profit in a number of ways, either by providing for groups of people to come to your home in the country to learn whatever you have to offer or by using other premises to do the same. There are many opportunities to offer your

subject specialism to residential colleges which will do all the marketing and administration, leaving you to simply enjoy the teaching aspect.

Languages for business

If your subject is foreign languages you could profit from the inevitable development of European links by offering to teach intensive business courses to local firms involved in import and export.

Craft workshops

The crafts are becoming increasingly popular both as a retreat from the sterility of mass-produced values and as a relaxing, leisure-time activity. Running workshops in almost any area of crafts should be popular.

Skills training

The need for skills training of all kinds is growing, so re-examine the skills you have and assess the likely opportunities for offering training in them.

Speaking, lecturing and demonstrating

There is an insatiable demand for good, interesting speakers and lecturers for all sorts of groups, clubs and societies. While these may not provide continuity of employment, they do offer an earning opportunity in their own right as well as acting as a showcase for your talents which may lead to further teaching or tutoring work.

Audio-visual presentations

Many subjects lend themselves to the creation of interesting slide and sound presentations, the beauty of which, apart from their intrinsic attractiveness, is that once you have put it together, the work involved in presenting it over and over again is nominal. Those with skills in creating audio-visual presentations could earn by putting them together for others on a professional basis.

Specialist vocational schools

A development which has taken place in America (where else?) is the growth of specialist private vocational schools such as training schools for chauffeurs, butlers, waiters and the like. What opportunities are there in your area – or, indeed, nationwide?

Children's summer camps

Again, an American idea which has taken root over here and where the demand is increasing. In the light of recent tragedies in outward bound type schools, you must plan to take the health and safety issues very seriously and run any such venture with the highest degree of professionalism.

Qualification-based courses

The range of qualifications available through schools and colleges is necessarily limited. What qualification-based courses could you offer or organise that are not being provided for in your community?

Training for small firms

While it may be tough to break into training for large organisations, there are many small businesses which have training needs which are not readily provided for. Talk to your local Chamber of Commerce or conduct a survey to find out what the needs are. Find a way to provide for these needs, delivering them in a form and at a time that suits the target clientele.

Distance learning

This is another growth area, as people find it increasingly difficult to commit themselves to regular attendance at a college or similar course. Why not write your own correspondence course and sell it by mail order?

Selling used correspondence courses

Here is an easy way for those with less marketable teaching skills. Buy second-hand correspondence courses (which are usually in good condition, as people rarely finish them) and sell or hire them out to keen new students.

Audio tapes

With the general decline in reading, audio tapes are becoming the preferred form of learning, as they can be listened to in the car while driving to and from work or on longer journeys. You could seek out suppliers of a range of educational tapes or record your own in your specialist subject (or get others to record their subject for you).

Video instruction

Likewise video is the great medium of today and instructional videos in all sorts of subjects are popular. It is amazing how careful planning and use of a simple camcorder can produce a very acceptable instruction video and the mark-up is very profitable.

Writing
If you are a specialist in teaching a particular subject, don't forget that writing about it can be a profitable spin-off. Not only does it increase your income, but it increases your professional standing as well, whether you are writing books or articles for magazines.

Educational consultancy
Educational consultancy is also a growth area, particularly as support services are being cut in education. This is an area where you can offer a wide range of support services to both children and adults on a fee-paying basis. There is also scope for specialist consultancy services for schools.

Saturday college
Many school pupils in the private sector are used to going to school on a Saturday morning and it is becoming an accepted way to enhance skills and knowledge more generally. A Saturday college could be for adults or children and could be leisure based or be seen as an extension of week-day education.

Open learning network
After the Open University and the Open College comes the Open Learning Network – yours! You could organise for people to teach others in a co-operative network where all that people pay is a membership fee that goes to the organiser – you! There are many variations on this idea.

English as a second/foreign language
This is another growth area, particularly the second, as more people come here from other countries and need to improve their English to survive. Indeed a great many people come to this country specifically to learn or to improve their English.

Educational books
Not only could you consider writing educational books, but there are many opportunities to become an agent for the sale of a wide range of books both to parents of children and to schools. Look in the business opportunity press for details.

Organising educational trips

As popular as learning holidays, if not more so, the clientele for educational and cultural trips is enormous and includes both foreign visitors and the vast majority of the indigenous population. Think of forty people on a coach trip to the theatre with a meal and your £5–£7.50 a head incorporated into the overall fee! There could be additional profit in negotiating a reduced group fee for the restaurant or the theatre too.

Services for teachers

Teachers are harassed and overburdened with paperwork, marking and all sorts of other responsibilities. Are there services you could offer them which would make their job easier? Alternatively, are there services you could offer them apart from their professional needs, as an easily targeted group with known needs and preferences?

Lesson preparation service

One such service could be a lesson preparation service, particularly if a series of lesson outlines could be provided to meet the needs of aspects of the National Curriculum, with the teachers being able to fill out the outline themselves to personalise the teaching.

Services to schools

Schools, too, have a requirement for services which were formerly supplied or looked after by the local authority. Some of these services could be supplied by an administrative member of staff which perhaps the school cannot afford. Perhaps you could organise them on a fee basis or act as a 'finder' on a commission basis of some kind.

Counselling

Counselling is a kind of teaching – helping people learn how to cope with personal situations and stresses. With basic training you could offer a service to schools for pupils and staff on an individual basis.

Running an independent study centre

Many people have skills to teach and contacts to whom they can teach them, but have no place to carry out their teaching. Could you set up an independent study centre where such people could rent a room by the hour or by the day, while you use some of the space for your own tutoring activities?

CASE STUDIES

Jim and Maggie share their birds

Having trained as an ornithologist and botanist respectively, Jim and Maggie live with their children, hens and several goats in a rambling old house on the moors, offering bed and breakfast to passers-by. They realised that they could capitalise on their beautiful situation and their expertise by running bird watching holidays. They have now added other subjects, including wild flowers and exploring prehistoric remains.

Alec offers talks

Alec took early retirement from his job as a teacher and combined his teaching skills with two of his hobbies, photography and history, to put together a well-illustrated slide talk (actually a very professional audio-visual presentation with music) which he now takes around the county giving talks to groups and societies for a fee. He has now developed several follow-up presentations of a similar kind to capitalise on the repeat business his shows generate.

Derek offers 'Edutainment' tapes

Another ex-teacher, Derek has developed a series of audio tapes through which children can learn some of the duller facts of life – like multiplication tables – by putting them to catchy music and selling them by mail order to schools and parents.

Saturday school franchise

Primary teacher Mary realised on her early retirement that there was a need for additional support for many children falling behind at school, so she started her own Saturday School which was so successful that she has now franchised the idea, with Saturday Schools beginning to spring up all over the country.

Maisie and Peter get booked up

When her husband Peter was made redundant, Maisie began to explore business ideas to find something they could build together and came across Dorling Kindersley Family Network. Dorling Kindersley, a big name in the publishing world, had developed a network marketing arm to introduce their quality books to parents and to schools. Maisie and Peter are doing well and have built up a team of distributors which is now earning them more than Peter earned before his redundancy. 'There's nothing like running your own business,' says Peter, 'Especially with the backing of such a prestigious company with so many excellent products.'

Verity and Jean start a magazine

Verity had a varied educational career behind her in schools and adult education and had also done educational consultancy work with the EU. Seeing a gap in the market she teamed up with printer Jean to run a new magazine focusing on the services schools have to buy in. The profits come from advertisers keen to access their specialist market.

9
Marketing Your Way to Success

Marketing is the key to the success of any business – assuming that the product or service is of sound quality. It is noticeable that it is not always the best product that captures the lion's share of the market, but the one which is marketed most effectively.

WHAT, EXACTLY, IS MARKETING?

Marketing covers everything
Marketing is not just another word for selling, though, of course, the two are closely connected. Marketing encompasses the whole concept of a business and its product(s):

• what kind of product (cheap or dear, big or small, the materials it is made from and so on)

• the people aimed at as customers (up-market, down-market, everybody, a particular group of people etc.)

• how it is envisaged the product or service will reach the end consumer (will it be sold directly from the company's own showrooms, sold to retailers, distributed by wholesalers, sold by direct mail or mail order adverts in newspapers and magazines or sold by a network of agents, perhaps by multi-level-marketing?).

Is there a market for your service?
Every aspect of the business, every decision that has to be made at the outset should be **marketing driven**. Otherwise you can end up with the common situation of a company trying to sell a new product or service for which there is not really a market. It may seem a brilliant idea to the owner of the company but he finds that not enough people are interested in buying it, or it is too expensive to reach them with his message, or the product itself is too expensive – there are all sorts of reasons why some things just don't work in the reality of the marketplace.

So, how do you avoid that sort of dead end when setting up your freelance teaching and tutoring business?

By thinking like a marketer, that's how.

SURVEYING THE MARKET

The starting point is to have a good look at the market you plan to enter. What is already there? Which education-type enterprises are doing well and which seem to be doing badly? Does the service you plan to offer already exist? If it doesn't, you may be onto a good thing, but think: if it doesn't exist, does it mean no-one wants it, that there is no demand? It seems unlikely that you will have been the first to think of that particular service.

Have a look, too, at other areas and see if a service similar to the one you plan exists. It could be that you have something to offer which is so new no one has ever thought of it before, but this is unlikely. On the other hand, don't be disheartened if you find your idea is already on sale in the marketplace. That proves that there is at least a demand and there may well be room in the market for you and your product or service, particularly if you offer it in an unusual or more effective way. Very often it is the subsequent entrants to a market who make the real money after a pioneer has spent the money in research and development to establish that there is a market need.

Try some basic **market research**. How? Ask around. Ask your friends and acquaintances. Get a clipboard, devise a simple questionnaire and ask people in the street. (Never fully believe what they tell you, but it might give you some indicators.)

PLANNING A MARKETING STRATEGY

Before you can draw up a marketing plan you have to have at least some idea of the answers to some basic questions, even if they are only your own assumptions at this point. Questions like:

- Who are my customers going to be?
- Where are they?
- What age, class, sex etc. are they?
- How can I contact them?
- Can I reach them through existing agencies?

- What is the competition offering?

- What exactly, are their needs?

- How can I tailor what I am offering to meet these needs?

- Where will they expect such provision to be made?

- How much will they be willing to pay?

Once you have an idea of some likely answers to these questions you can begin to put together a marketing strategy. For example, let's say that:

- Your customers are likely to be young business people.

- They work in the commercial centre of your nearest big town.

- They are likely to be middle class, grammar school educated and between the ages of 20 and 40.

- They could be reached by mailshots to the large companies where they work and by ads in the local paper's career section.

- You might decide to approach the local branches of the Institute of Directors, the Institute of Management and similar organisations to propose some kind of joint venture.

- The competition is likely to be the local FE college or university offering short courses in the evening or one-year full-time courses.

- Their needs may be for a flexible learning system that they can fit into the rest of their lives, choosing their own times to study.

- You may decide that what you need to offer is a flexible learning environment with self-study units backed by informal lunch-time sessions held in company premises by arrangement with the management, a telephone helpline evenings and weekends, and optional Saturday or Sunday schools.

- Their expectations will be conventional, so the idea of a course operating in a radically different way from a traditional college course may need to be sold to them.

- Perception of price often relates to how they see the value of the course. If you present it in an easy-to-pay structure you may well find that there is no real price barrier. 'Payment is by standing order at £25 a month over 18 months seems very reasonable compared to a blunt 'The course fee is £450'.

Your marketing strategy should be capable of clear expression in a paragraph of a hundred words or so. Of course, when you begin to plan in detail how to carry it out, it will cover several sheets of paper. It will need to cover costing as well. It may seem obvious that your ideal marketing medium is advertising on television, but that is usually (though not always) prohibitive to all but substantial businesses, so you may have to be content with the less than ideal newspaper or radio ads instead. However, it is good to know that you can identify the ideal way forwards even if it seems beyond your budget at present.

UNIQUE SELLING PROPOSITION (USP)

Before you begin to think about advertising try to identify what marketing people call your Unique Selling Proposition (USP). In other words, what is the one thing that makes your business, product or service different from (and by implication better than) the competition? It could be price, quality, unique style of delivery, biggest, smallest, most caring or any other aspect that distinguishes you from others. Once identified, that should be the focal point of all your advertising and promotion.

ADVERTISING

There are few businesses that can flourish without advertising of some sort. However, it is good to bear in mind Lord Lever's famous remark that half of his advertising was a waste of money – if only he knew which half, he would have been a great deal richer!

It is easy to lose a great deal of money advertising. Some of the following may help you to avoid at least some of that waste.

How much to spend

First, decide on an advertising budget for your business within your general business plan. Of course, it is hard to come up with hard and fast rules, but a general rule of thumb seems to be that you should expect your advertising budget to be around one-fifth to a third of the income it generates. Thus, if you want to pull in £60,000 in a year, you might well have to spend somewhere between £12,000 to £20,000 to achieve that. That may seem a lot, but bear in mind that you will not be spending all that right at the start, but at the rate of £230 to £380 a week, and much of it will be paid from income that the advertising generates. There are, however, ways of advertising which cost a great deal less. These are discussed later in this chapter.

Making your advertising work

Before you think of splashing out on huge display adverts, start off by learning to use the classified advertising columns. Here the secret is to use the shortest possible message to evoke a response such as sending or phoning for further information. Compare the following two adverts:

> NEW TUTOR offers tuition in clarinet and saxophone. Both classical and popular styles catered for. My rates are very competitive at £10 per hour and I can offer tuition at your home or mine. Please ring between 4pm and 6pm to arrange suitable times. Tel: (0000) 777777.

> SAX & CLARINET PLAYERS – I can have you playing professionally in just 20 weeks! Phone for details (0000) 777777 (24 hours).

Notice that the second ad is only 21 words compared to the 47 of the first one, so it will make your advertising budget go further. What is more, it obeys the prime rule of advertising where the first ad breaks it: it focuses on the customer and his or her needs, not on the provider and his or her service. It also focuses on the benefit the reader will get from the service. And, because the second advertiser has invested in a low-cost answer-phone, the convenience factor makes it far easier to respond. Which ad would you reply to?

Figure 9 outlines some basic rules of good advertisement writing.

Display advertising

Experiment with classified ads to find out what works before even thinking of paying for display advertising. If you do decide to move up to display advertising remember that the ideal place for a display advert is in the first half of the paper at the top, preferably right-hand corner of a right-hand page. Of course the newspaper people know this, so they are not likely to offer you that good position easily. Learn to be tough – demand it. Be a difficult customer to sell to, even if you know that you want to take the advertising anyway.

How to buy advertising space cheaply

Here is another way to get advertising cheaply. Plan the advert you want to use. Prepare it so that it is available in various sizes, then let the advertisement salesperson know that you are in the market for **remnant space**. This is where there may be an ad space left at the

Good advertising follows the structure of the basic sales presentation, expressed in the **AIDA** formula:

A for Attention
I for Interest
D for Desire
A for Action

So, a good advert will start with a bang to grab the attention. How do you do that? By immediately focusing on the most interesting thing in the world. What is that? **You**, of course! There is nothing more interesting to anyone than themselves and their own concerns, so start with the word 'you' and follow it with something of enormous benefit to the person addressed. Alternatively, start with the second most powerful word in advertising, 'free'. Better still, use both:

YOU can have a FREE sax or clarinet lesson. Learn to be a STAR! Phone NOW to arrange it! (0000) 777777.

That advert attracts my **attention** because it speaks to me. It qualifies the response by screening out anyone not interested in playing an instrument. The free offer grabs my **interest** and feeds my **desire** for fame and fortune. Equally important – it asks for **action** by telling me what I have to do **now**! And at, say, 30p a word, it would only cost £6.30!

Remember to focus all your advertising on the 'you' message rather than the 'me' message. Use the ordinary, friendly language of speech rather than stiffer, more formal language.

Make your message different so that it stands out but don't go for gimmicks that don't home in on the essential message you want to get across.

Finally, every advert asking people to write to you should be coded so that you can tell how many responses you are getting from an advert in a particular paper or magazine. For example, '(Dept. C71096)'will tell you that the advert appeared in the *Courier* in the week beginning 7 October 1996.

Fig. 9. How to write ads that work.

end of the day or week or month just before going to press and it will often be sold at 50 per cent discount or more. If they offer it to you for 25 per cent off, counter-offer with a 50 per cent offer. If they offer it to you at 50 per cent, counter-offer with 75 per cent – you may get it for 35 per cent or 65 per cent respectively.

Another way to gain from **remnant offers** is this. If you know that the going rate for the space you want to buy is say, £120, write an undated cheque for the amount you want to pay for that space – £30, £50 or whatever – and send in your copy with the undated cheque and a letter that reads something like:

> Dear Mr Blob
>
> I know that you sometimes find yourself with a late cancellation or a space that is left over just prior to going to press.
>
> I am enclosing my undated cheque for £XX on the understanding that you may keep this until such a situation arises and run the enclosed copy to fill the space.
>
> If you do not wish to accept this offer perhaps you would return my cheque at your convenience.
>
> Yours sincerely
> Jim Bargainhunter

Advert design

Try to design your display adverts so that they leap out from the page to seize the reader by the throat. Your advert could be round in shape, for example, or it could start with the word 'FREE' in huge letters. A visual image helps, and while it should be related to the message, research shows that a human face is the most effective, starting with a female face, followed by a child's face, with mere males last in order of preference. Get hold of a book of copyright-free artwork and see if there are any appealing images that spark off ideas that you can use to develop a good advert.

Don't try to cram everything into your advert. Leave some attractive white space around the text and think about what you are trying to achieve. What is it you want the reader to do after he or she has read your advert?

FREE ADVERTISING

Being a Scot, I don't like paying out any money for advertising at all – and generally, I don't have to. Why? Because I get my advertising free in one of two ways.

Press releases

The first of these is to get newspapers and magazines to run items about me and my business free. I do this by sending out press releases to appropriate magazines and newspapers when I can think of something newsworthy they might be interested in. That could be information about a new product – a new nutritional product that enables you to eat fatty foods without getting fat, for example.

The most mundane things can often provide an 'angle' you can hang a story on and sometimes you can make news happen by staging an event or issuing a controversial statement or publication.

A brilliant way that never fails is to write and print a short report related to your business and offer it free to readers. Not only does this get your business free publicity, it will get you lots of qualified prospects who can be sent details of your service along with the free report. Better still, when you send them the report with a covering letter and details of your business, invite them to call and inspect your business, have a chat, get some free advice and send them a voucher for £5 off when they decide to become a customer.

Your press release should be no longer than a single sheet, double spaced, and should contain all the important information in the first sentence. It should have your name and telephone number at the foot so that you can be contacted for further information.

Exchange articles for adverts

The second way to get free advertising is to write articles relating to the area in which you do business and offer them to papers and magazines on the basis that they can use them free as long as they either offer you a free advert in exchange or, at the very least, tag on a paragraph at the end of the article advising readers how to get in touch with you for further help.

This is a technique I use all the time. For example, a short article on writing is followed by basic information about my book, *Earn £180 a Day Writing*, including the fact that it can be obtained for £15 post free from me at the address given.

My regular syndicated articles appear in lots of small business opportunity magazines which run a free advert for whatever aspect of my business I am promoting at the time. A recent article in *Business Opportunity Digest*, for example, brought me in around 160 requests for more information about the business that was the subject of the article.

KEEP MARKETING AT THE FOREFRONT OF YOUR MIND

Always be thinking of ways to promote your business and bring it to the attention of the public and, in particular, to convey the message of what benefits your business can bring to your prospective clients.

Let me take this opportunity, as an example, to invite you to contact me for information about a specialist marketing course I am able to offer which will be helpful to anyone marketing a business of any kind. Ask for details of 'Your Marketing Genius on Tape' and write to:

John Wilson
Business Innovations Research
Tregeraint House
Zennor, St Ives
Cornwall, TR26 3DB
Tel/Fax: (01736) 797061

CASE STUDIES

Tom's three marketing strands

When Tom set up his outdoor pursuits centre he was fortunate to have a bank manager who understood the key role of marketing and insisted Tom's business plan outlined a comprehensive marketing strategy.

Tom set aside a budget of £3,000 in the first year and deployed most of that in taking small display adverts in various management magazines. He sent mailshots every three months to the larger firms in his locality and paid a local writer to put together a series of press releases and stories based on his more colourful exploits as a sergeant in the Marines. These were sent to local, regional and national papers and resulted in a number of features being published.

Tom has also built into his marketing a referral system where participants on his courses are asked to identify three or four colleagues who would benefit from Tom's courses. Before they leave the course Tom's secretary has typed out personalised copies of a standard letter of recommendation for them to sign.

Linda is never short of students

Officially, the responsibility for the marketing of Linda's jam-making classes lies with the adult education centres where she teaches.

However, Linda is aware that if not enough students are attracted the classes will not run and she will lose income, so she does her own marketing, although she does not recognise it as such.

Several weeks before enrolment begins for adult education classes, Linda writes to all her former students telling them of the classes she is offering in the forthcoming adult education programmes. She also sends a notice out to all the local Women's Institute and Townswomen's Guild branches and offers to give talks to these and other groups throughout the year. As she still makes and sells her own jam she gives out a leaflet about her classes with every jar she sells. Linda is never short of students for her classes.

Elaine and Eddie's strategy

Elaine and Eddie's tutorial business is now well established in its own premises in town. They chose the site of their office very carefully so that they could have a highly visible sign both at street level by the entrance and high up on the wall. The side window also displays an attractive dayglo poster. They have a regular series of adverts with the local paper and have an arrangement to run a weekly article related to education and jobs which ties in with promoting their tutorial business.

CHECKLIST

1. How far have you surveyed the local market in your area to see what is already on offer?

2. Do you have a clear idea of who your customers are likely to be and where and how you will find them?

3. Work out what you consider would be an appropriate advertising budget for your enterprise and detail how this would be spent.

4. What could you do to get free publicity for your business?

5. Try writing a series of classified ads for your business aimed at persuading people to take specific action.

6. Draft a couple of display adverts you could use in appropriate papers and journals.

7. Write the text of a standard letter you might send to prospective

students along with information about what your business offers them.

8. If you already have printed information prepared for your business, review it to see how far it obeys the rules for good advertising as detailed in this chapter. Does it stress benefits? Is it client-centred rather than focused on you and your business?

10
Building Up Your Business

Your aim may be simply to pick up some part-time teaching work as a freelance teacher or tutor working within the local authority system or the private sector. Or it may be to build an independent educational business of your own. Whatever your goals, you will need to plan ahead for the future growth and development of your business – or simply its continuance. It is undoubtedly the case that if your business ceases to grow and develop it will in all likelihood wither away and die.

This final chapter, which is strongly related to the marketing theme of the previous one, addresses some of the issues you need to consider to ensure the long-term success of your freelance teaching and tutoring business.

WHAT DO CUSTOMERS COST?

Because people starting new businesses of any kind have to start from scratch and spend a great deal of time and energy looking for their first customers, they tend to get into the mind-set of spending the majority of their efforts seeking out new customers.

Finding a constant supply of new customers is an important component of success, but if it is the sole focus then the business is destined to fail – unless it is a very specialist business in which, by the nature of the product or service, a customer can only be a customer once – and there are, in reality, very few businesses like that.

The reason why businesses that are always pursuing new customers will inevitably fail is that it is such an expensive business that the resulting sale is rarely worth the effort involved – it is rarely profitable. Research suggests that it costs something like seven to ten times as much to win a new customer as to sell to an existing customer. A business which is wholly dependent on gaining new customers all the time is not only a very pressurised business, but one in which costs are very high.

Typically, a sales representative will have to call on a new prospect around eight times before winning any business from them. A typical mail shot to a list of potential buyers will be doing well if it results in two sales from every hundred letters. An advert costing £150 may pull in just five customers spending £35 each, perhaps covering the cost of the advert and some of the overheads – break-even, or a small loss.

EXISTING CUSTOMERS ARE MORE PROFITABLE

Target existing customers

It follows from this that the successful business is one which makes the most of existing customers and most businesses, unless they are ones where customers come back automatically – like a shop or a garage – don't do nearly enough marketing to their existing customers. Even shops and garages and similar businesses could increase their business enormously by creating a marketing policy which targets existing customers.

Repeat business is the key to profits

Existing customers are so valuable because they are known consumers of what your business is offering. What is more, having bought from you once, they will be happy to do business with you again – provided, of course, that you have given them satisfaction (and even more so if you have given them super-satisfaction). And, of course, you know who they are, where they are and what they have bought from you in the past. These are factors on which you can build profitable repeat business. This is known in marketing terms as 'back-end sales', particularly profitable because the cost of selling them is so low compared with the cost of selling the same service to a completely new customer who has to be found by expensive advertising or other means.

Keeping a mailing list

It is surprising how few 'ordinary' (as distinct from specifically mail order) businesses make a record of customers' names and addresses or telephone numbers or what they buy. The average small business thinks it is doing a good job simply by running an advert in the local paper making its special offers and all will be well. It might be, but it would do considerably better if it were to send a letter to existing customers acknowledging their past custom and making them an offer only available to them as preferred customers. That offer could be made by enclosing a £5 or £10 voucher redeemable against their next purchase provided it is made within, say, the next ten days.

Making an offer

There is no reason why you should not get more business by using the same methods, adapted to the client base for your services and the product or service you are offering. You could offer a college principal a couple of free day schools providing he or she offers your twenty-week class in the main programme. You could offer twelve lessons for the price of ten or an additional summer school at half price to those who sign up for a specified number of tuition sessions. Use your imagination. Make an offer.

Creating new products

Most one-product businesses are fundamentally weak, so think about what else you could be offering to existing customers. This could be a variant of the subject you first choose to offer or a new angle on the subject. It could be a new, preferably related subject:

- a teacher of drawing and painting could add art appreciation or print making to her repertoire

- the driving tutor could offer a basic course in 'Looking After Your Car'

- students of French would be happy to sign up for complementary courses on 'Understanding France', 'The Wines of France' or 'Planning Your Holiday in France'.

Ancillary products

Don't forget that additional products could be items related to the teaching or tutoring rather than further teaching or tutoring.

- Could you buy the textbooks wholesale and get 35-50 per cent profit on selling them on to the students?

- Could you deal in new and second-hand musical instruments for your music students to purchase?

- Could you arrange trips to Spain and elsewhere for language students?

What, in short, are the related needs of your students which you could supply for profit?

DEVELOPING THROUGH TRAINING

While the knowledge and skills you have now may be sufficient for you to flourish as a freelance teacher or tutor, it is important for you to keep up to date with your subject and with new developments both in that field and in the field of education and training generally.

Bear in mind, too, that by undertaking further training you can extend the range and scope of your skills so that you are able to offer more to your clientele as a teacher and tutor. Always be aware of what opportunities are available for you to invest in yourself, at both local and national level.

DEVELOPING THROUGH VOLUME

There is a natural limit to what one person can achieve, particularly if operating in a one-to-one business like personal tutoring. There are several ways in which you can increase the volume and therefore the profitability of your business.

Teaching in small groups

An obvious way to increase your productivity is to teach in small groups rather than one-to-one. This has, as has been pointed out in an earlier chapter, a number of advantages, including increasing the hourly rate of fees you can collect, reducing the cost to the students and releasing more of your time from the 'coal face' of teaching to the developmental aspects of your business like marketing so that you can make it grow even more.

Taking on staff

In business it has always been the case that the person who makes the most money is the person who manages the work of others. By taking on staff (on a casual, part-time basis according to demand) and by combining this with small group tuition, your business could become very profitable indeed, particularly as the range of subjects you are able to offer your clientele will be far greater than the limitations of your own subject expertise.

If teaching one person brings in £10 an hour and teaching five brings in £35 an hour, then three tutors, teaching groups of five (and being paid £12 an hour) will bring in £69 an hour – and all the hours they are making that money for you leave you free to work on developing more business!

Franchising your operation

If you have developed a system of teaching or a tutoring agency which has proved to be successful and has a good administrative and marketing structure, it might pay you to consider franchising as an alternative to opening additional branches of your own enterprise. The advantage is that it obviates the need for large capital injections to establish each new branch. On the contrary, it injects large capital sums into *your* business. In addition, it provides a growing source of revenue from franchise fees based on a proportion of the new outlets' business volume. If your system is based on particular teaching materials, the sale of these could form a further stream of revenue.

Before considering franchising your enterprise, think about what is unique about it that will lend itself to developing a distinctive franchise image. Make sure that you have at least one additional successful branch up and running to prove that your system is transferable and will work in other areas when run by other people. Take professional advice from qualified franchise advisers when you are ready to take this step.

CASE STUDIES

Tom tailors his training

Tom is fortunate in that his 'outward bound' type courses are sold to reasonably large companies where there is always a pool of junior, middle and senior managers to come on his courses. Once the company has used his services, they will continue to provide new clients. Tom has also actively marketed the idea of similar courses for employees at every level and tailored special courses for particular groups. These are, again, being sold to his existing client group of companies, so Tom's marketing costs are low and his profitability high.

Jim and Maggie mail twice a year

Jim and Maggie's bird-watching, flower and pre-history courses take place largely in the summer, as does the bed and breakfast side of their business. Around January/February they mail out a letter with details of their courses to everyone who has been on their courses or stopped for bed and breakfast.

Recently they realised that they could increase their business by offering winter courses focused on indoor activities and have recruited other local people with skills to offer to supplement their own. They now do a second mailing around September with details of courses on 'Writing', 'Assertiveness for Women' and 'Music Making'.

Alec develops new products

As well as developing new subjects for his talks to groups and societies, Alec has printed up some of the period photographs which form part of his slide presentation and sells copies for a few pounds at each talk he gives. He is now putting together a book on his local area to complement his local history talks which should also sell well at his talks and, as it will be self-published, even a few sales will net a useful additional income.

Elaine and Eddie have big plans

With the successful growth of their tutorial business, Eddie and Elaine realised that they had a winning formula and are in discussion with a specialist firm of franchise advisers with a view to setting up a network of franchised outlets throughout the country. In preparation for this they have appointed a manager for the original agency and are working with a second manager on opening another trial branch in a nearby town.

CHECKLIST

1. Try to analyse the cost of gaining a new client. You could simply total up all your advertising and promotional costs and divide the result by the number of clients you have. Work out, by contrast, what it would cost to send a mailshot to these existing customers two or three times a year, bearing in mind that the response should be at least several times that of a similar mailing to new potential customers.

2. Draw up a list of possible additional products or services you could sell to your existing client base and begin to develop them in order of priority.

3. What special offer could you make to existing or past customers on your mailing list? Draft a sales letter making that offer and design a voucher to accompany the offer and make it attractive to them.

4. In what direction could you extend your own skills so that you have more to offer as a freelance tutor and teacher? Where could you obtain the necessary training? What developments are taking place in your subject or in education and training that you need to be aware of?

5. Who do you know of that you could invite to tutor for you either in your own subject area or in complementary areas? Is there enough demand in your marketplace to begin to aim for more volume in this way? What potential has your enterprise for turning into a franchise operation?

Further Reading

The Student Teacher's Handbook, Christine Edwards and Maura Healy (Kogan Page).

Running Your Own Playgroup or Nursery, Jenny Willison (Kogan Page).

Year Book of Adult Continuing Education: a Directory of Organisations (NIACE).

The Adult Learner – A Neglected Species, Malcolm Knowles (Gulf Publishing Company).

Freedom to Learn, Carl Rogers and H. Jerome Freiberg (Merrill).

Resources for Teachers of Adults, John Cummins (NIACE).

Learning from Experience, Wilma Fraser (NIACE).

Tutoring, John C. Miller (Further Education Unit).

Understanding How People Learn, David G. Reay (Kogan Page).

Lifelong Learning, Norman Longworth and W. Keith Davies (Kogan Page).

Improving Your Students' Learning, Alastair Morgan (Kogan Page).

Teaching Through Projects, Jane Henry (Kogan Page).

Assessing Students, Derek Rowntree (Kogan Page).

Learning in Groups, David Jaques (Kogan Page).

Producing Teaching Materials, Henry Ellington and Phil Race (Kogan Page).

500 Tips for Tutors, Phil Race and Sally Brown (Kogan Page).

Everything You Ever Needed to Know About Training, Kaye Thorne and David Mackey (Kogan Page).

The Effective Use of Role Play, Morry van Ments (Kogan Page).

How To Start Your Own Business, Jim Green (How To Books).

Going Freelance, Godfrey Golzen (Granada).

How To Market Yourself, Ian Phillipson (How To Books).

Marketing Services, John Courtis (BIM/Kogan Page).

Writing a CV That Works, Paul McGee (How To Books).

Simple Cash Books For Small Businesses, Paul D. Ordidge (Kogan Page).

How To Do Your Own Advertising, Michael Bennie (How To Books).

How To Do Your Own PR, Ian Phillipson (How To Books).

How to Write Sales Letters That Sell, Drayton Bird (Kogan Page).

The Secrets of Effective Direct Mail, John Fraser-Robinson (McGraw Hill).

Adults Learning (a monthly journal) (NIACE).

Glossary

Adult education. Day and evening classes for recreational and non-vocational subjects run by local education authorities, universities, the Workers Educational Association and residential colleges.

Aims and objectives. A phrase used with some vagueness of definition in education. Aims define the general purpose of a course while objectives can be seen as more specific and measurable achievements.

Brainstorming. A technique of throwing up lots of ideas uncritically for later evaluation.

Case studies. Real or fictional people or situations which show how things would work out in practice.

Correspondence course. A course sent by mail in parts, usually involving the return of exercises assessed by a tutor.

Demonstration. A teaching method where a process is done by the tutor for students to see how it is done.

Direct mail. Marketing by mailing a letter, usually accompanied by a brochure and a reply envelope or card. Often disparagingly known as 'junk mail'.

Discovery learning. A teaching process in which students learn by exploration, trial and error and experiment.

Discussion. A teaching method based on controlled discussion and argument, often structured and directed by the tutor towards exploring or revealing certain ideas or principles.

Distance learning. Any kind of learning or teaching which is not face-to-face but based on radio, TV, correspondence etc.

Empowerment. The concept of letting students be in control of their own learning, of taking charge rather than being dependent on the tutor.

Enabling. The idea of the tutor as someone who helps the student towards **independent learning** rather than controlling the learning process.

Extra-mural department. The department of a university which takes university-level study outside the university into the community (literally 'outside the walls').

Further education. Usually refers to vocational and technical education provided from the age of 16 upwards in colleges which are seen as being of a lower educational level of post-school education than universities and polytechnics.

Goals. Specific personal or business targets to aim for.

Group work. In educational terms this refers to the process of working with small numbers of people, usually between three and a dozen. The optimum size of a group is thought to be about seven people.

Higher education. The sector of education comprising universities, polytechnics, art colleges and some other specialist colleges.

Independent learning. Learning that is accomplished without the aid of a tutor, course or teaching institution.

Learning. The process of discovering and absorbing new knowledge or skills.

Learning experience. Any experience which provides new learning.

Lecture. A lengthy exposition of a subject given by one person to an audience in a formal setting.

Leisure learning. Usually refers to adult education type classes and courses in recreational and hobby subjects.

Lesson plan. The organisation of what is to be taught into a cohesive structure with a method of presentation.

Life-long learning. The idea that learning is not confined to the period spent at school or college but is a process that goes on throughout life.

Local education authority. The local council, usually county or metropolitan, responsible for state educational provision.

Mail order. The marketing of goods and services by mail, usually through placing advertisements in newspapers and magazines.

Mail shot. The package sent in a **direct mail** campaign, consisting of a letter, a brochure and a response device such as a reply envelope or card.

Mixed ability teaching. Usually regarded as a form of social engineering replacing rigid streaming of pupils in school into supposedly cohesive intellectual groups. Mixed ability teaching is, in fact, the norm, as variations in aptitude and experience make the learning process different for almost every individual.

National Curriculum. A recent introduction, the National Curriculum consists of a series of closely defined teaching objectives which must be covered in the school curriculum.

Open College. Following the success of the Open University, the Open College was set up to provide **distance learning** at a lower level in a wide variety of largely vocational subjects.

Open learning. Any system of learning to which access is not restricted by the holding of prior qualifications.

Open University. A highly innovative **distance learning** system linked to national media and using correspondence and summer schools as well as local tutorial support to bring university-level education to those without prior qualification and whose circumstances preclude attendance on a full-time university course.

Private school. Also known confusingly in the UK as public schools, a better name is independent schools, that is, schools not supported by the state (except in terms of reliefs given to charitable bodies, which most are) where education is paid for by fees.

Problem-solving. In educational terms a teaching method where principles are learned through tackling and solving specifically posed problems.

Project work. A form of learning where the emphasis is on finding out and presenting information (either study-based or experience-based) involving personal initiative, choice and presentation.

Role play. Learning by acting out parts and situations to increase understanding of issues, emotions and decision-making.

Rote learning. Learning parrot fashion. While over-used in the past it still has a useful role in helping students to retain factual information.

Seminar. A study session usually of one day's duration which may include a variety of presentations on a specialist subject or area.

Simulation. An educational exercise where an event or situation is set up as if it were real and the processes and experience worked through to increase understanding of events or what lies behind them.

Special needs. A wide range of educational disadvantage is covered by this term – the hard of hearing, the visually impaired, the educationally subnormal, the physically handicapped, school refusers etc.

State school. Any school run by public funding, usually under the control of a **local education authority**.

Student-centred learning. An educational approach which puts the learning needs of the students at the centre of the process.

Syllabus. Description in some detail of the contents of a course. Sometimes used to cover the whole programme of an educational institution (more properly a prospectus).

Teacher training. Teacher training for schools is usually offered as a four-year course covering both subjects and teaching methods in a specialist teacher training college or a department of a university. There is also a one-year course for graduates and a variety of part-time courses for teachers in further and adult education.

Teaching. It is important to distinguish the process of teaching (what the teacher does) from **learning** (what the student does). The one may not necessarily lead to the other, so attention should be focused on how far the teaching leads to learning on the part of the student.

Training. Usually distinguished from **teaching** as being a narrower discipline, having a purely vocational function.

Training and Enterprise Councils. The TECs are government agencies designed to bring together resources in local areas for training for the job market and self-employment.

Transferable skills. The concept that skills learned and practised in one area can be adapted for use in another area. Teachers, for example, could transfer their organisational and people skills to the area of general management.

Unique Selling Proposition. That feature of a business, product or service which makes it stand out as different from the competition.

VAT. A tax payable on the provision of any product or service (with certain exemptions) by any business with a business volume in excess of (currently) £47,000.

Whiteboard. A replacement of the old-fashioned chalk board, being a white plastic-surfaced board written on with spirit or water-based markers.

Worksheets. Sheets containing exercises or other work to be carried out by students.

Workshops. A term used for **seminar**-type sessions in which participation may include practical as well as verbal inputs by the students.

Index

HOW TO BE A FREELANCE SECRETARY
Your path to a more rewarding future

Leonie Luzak

Fed up with redundancy? Tired of temping? Want to improve your quality and standard of living? If you have the right basic keyboard and personal skills, you too could set up as a freelance secretary, earning double or treble the money you received as an employee, and with the satisfaction, self-respect and enhanced prospects of working for yourself. Instead of a boss, you have a client; instead of a wage you have a growing fees income; instead of commuting you can work from home. Leonie Luzak has herself — despite (or perhaps because of) the recession — made a great success in this field, and has written this informative step-by-step guide to answer the often-asked question, 'How did you do it?' Here's how!

144pp. illus. 1 85703 087 7.

CAREER PLANNING FOR WOMEN
How to make a positive impact on your working life

Laurel Alexander

More women are entering the workplace than ever before. Whether it is on the corporate ladder or self employed, women are establishing a much stronger place for themselves within the world of commerce and industry. As global and national markets shift and business ethos develops, the specific qualities of women play a vital part alongside those of men. Business has been influenced primarily by male thought and action. Now there is the opportunity for women to make a substantial contribution with new ideas and approaches. The book is not about women taking men's jobs or about women being better or worse than men. It is intended to help women understand their unique and emerging role in business, change their perception of themselves and take much more responsibility for their responses and actions within the workplace. Laurel Alexander is a manager/trainer in career development who has helped many individuals succeed in changing their work direction. She is also author of *Surviving Redundancy* in this series.

160pp. illus. 1 85703 417 1.

SURVIVING REDUNDANCY
How to take charge of yourself and your future

Laurel Alexander

When redundancy hits, you can either view the event as a horror story or as a challenge for positive growth. This book sets out in a helpful way how to survive the first few weeks, both practically and emotionally. It explains how to redefine your work motivations, how to create a professional jobsearch strategy and network your skills, how to approach self employment, contract and temporary work as well as educational and training options. The key to any successful career change is the right psychological attitude, and issues such as dealing with change and positive self talk are explained with case study examples. Laurel Alexander is a manager/trainer in career management who has helped many individuals succeed in changing their career direction.

156pp. illus. 1 85703 187 3.

HOW TO START A NEW CAREER
Managing a better future for yourself

Judith Johnstone

More people than ever before are faced with big career changes today. Few if any jobs are 'for life'. Now in its second edition, this How To book helps you manage your entry into a new career effectively. It is aimed at anyone making a new start, whatever his or her age or background. It looks at who you are and what you are. It helps you evaluate your life skills, to recognise which careers you should concentrate on, and how to make a realistic plan for a happy and productive future. 'Written very much in the style of a work book, with practical exercises and pro formas for the student to complete . . . Well written – would be a useful addition to the library of any guidance practitioner working with adults.' *Newscheck/Careers Service Bulletin.*

140pp. illus. 1 85703 139 3. 2nd edition

How To Books provide practical help on a large range of topics. They are available through all good bookshops or can be ordered direct from the distributors. Just tick the titles you want and complete the form on the following page.

___ Apply to an Industrial Tribunal (£7.99)	___ Getting That Job (£8.99)
___ Applying for a Job (£8.99)	___ Getting your First Job (£8.99)
___ Applying for a United States Visa (£15.99)	___ Going to University (£8.99)
___ Backpacking Round Europe (£8.99)	___ Helping your Child to Read (£8.99)
___ Be a Freelance Journalist (£8.99)	___ How to Study & Learn (£8.99)
___ Be a Freelance Secretary (£8.99)	___ Investing in People (£9.99)
___ Become a Freelance Sales Agent (£9.99)	___ Investing in Stocks & Shares (£9.99)
___ Become an Au Pair (£8.99)	___ Keep Business Accounts (£7.99)
___ Becoming a Father (£8.99)	___ Know Your Rights at Work (£8.99)
___ Buy & Run a Shop (£8.99)	___ Live & Work in America (£9.99)
___ Buy & Run a Small Hotel (£8.99)	___ Live & Work in Australia (£12.99)
___ Buying a Personal Computer (£9.99)	___ Live & Work in Germany (£9.99)
___ Career Networking (£8.99)	___ Live & Work in Greece (£9.99)
___ Career Planning for Women (£8.99)	___ Live & Work in Italy (£8.99)
___ Cash from your Computer (£9.99)	___ Live & Work in New Zealand (£9.99)
___ Choosing a Nursing Home (£9.99)	___ Live & Work in Portugal (£9.99)
___ Choosing a Package Holiday (£8.99)	___ Live & Work in the Gulf (£9.99)
___ Claim State Benefits (£9.99)	___ Living & Working in Britain (£8.99)
___ Collecting a Debt (£9.99)	___ Living & Working in China (£9.99)
___ Communicate at Work (£7.99)	___ Living & Working in Hong Kong (£10.99)
___ Conduct Staff Appraisals (£7.99)	___ Living & Working in Israel (£10.99)
___ Conducting Effective Interviews (£8.99)	___ Living & Working in Saudi Arabia (£12.99)
___ Coping with Self Assessment (£9.99)	___ Living & Working in the Netherlands (£9.99)
___ Copyright & Law for Writers (£8.99)	___ Making a Complaint (£8.99)
___ Counsel People at Work (£7.99)	___ Making a Wedding Speech (£8.99)
___ Creating a Twist in the Tale (£8.99)	___ Manage a Sales Team (£8.99)
___ Creative Writing (£9.99)	___ Manage an Office (£8.99)
___ Critical Thinking for Students (£8.99)	___ Manage Computers at Work (£8.99)
___ Dealing with a Death in the Family (£9.99)	___ Manage People at Work (£8.99)
___ Do Voluntary Work Abroad (£8.99)	___ Manage Your Career (£8.99)
___ Do Your Own Advertising (£8.99)	___ Managing Budgets & Cash Flows (£9.99)
___ Do Your Own PR (£8.99)	___ Managing Meetings (£8.99)
___ Doing Business Abroad (£10.99)	___ Managing Your Personal Finances (£8.99)
___ Doing Business on the Internet (£12.99)	___ Managing Yourself (£8.99)
___ Emigrate (£9.99)	___ Market Yourself (£8.99)
___ Employ & Manage Staff (£8.99)	___ Master Book-Keeping (£8.99)
___ Find Temporary Work Abroad (£8.99)	___ Mastering Business English (£8.99)
___ Finding a Job in Canada (£9.99)	___ Master GCSE Accounts (£8.99)
___ Finding a Job in Computers (£8.99)	___ Master Public Speaking (£8.99)
___ Finding a Job in New Zealand (£9.99)	___ Migrating to Canada (£12.99)
___ Finding a Job with a Future (£8.99)	___ Obtaining Visas & Work Permits (£9.99)
___ Finding Work Overseas (£9.99)	___ Organising Effective Training (£9.99)
___ Freelance DJ-ing (£8.99)	___ Pass Exams Without Anxiety (£7.99)
___ Freelance Teaching & Tutoring (£9.99)	___ Passing That Interview (£8.99)
___ Get a Job Abroad (£10.99)	___ Plan a Wedding (£7.99)
___ Get a Job in America (£9.99)	___ Planning Your Gap Year (£8.99)
___ Get a Job in Australia (£9.99)	___ Prepare a Business Plan (£8.99)
___ Get a Job in Europe (£9.99)	___ Publish a Book (£9.99)
___ Get a Job in France (£9.99)	___ Publish a Newsletter (£9.99)
___ Get a Job in Travel & Tourism (£8.99)	___ Raise Funds & Sponsorship (£7.99)
___ Get into Radio (£8.99)	___ Rent & Buy Property in France (£9.99)
___ Getting into Films & Television (£10.99)	___ Rent & Buy Property in Italy (£9.99)

___ Research Methods (£8.99)
___ Retire Abroad (£8.99)
___ Return to Work (£7.99)
___ Run a Voluntary Group (£8.99)
___ Setting up Home in Florida (£9.99)
___ Spending a Year Abroad (£8.99)
___ Start a Business from Home (£7.99)
___ Start a New Career (£6.99)
___ Starting to Manage (£8.99)
___ Starting to Write (£8.99)
___ Start Word Processing (£8.99)
___ Start Your Own Business (£8.99)
___ Study Abroad (£8.99)
___ Study & Live in Britain (£7.99)
___ Studying at University (£8.99)
___ Studying for a Degree (£8.99)
___ Successful Grandparenting (£8.99)
___ Successful Mail Order Marketing (£9.99)
___ Successful Single Parenting (£8.99)
___ Survive Divorce (£8.99)
___ Surviving Redundancy (£8.99)
___ Taking in Students (£8.99)
___ Taking on Staff (£8.99)
___ Taking Your A-Levels (£8.99)
___ Teach Abroad (£8.99)
___ Teach Adults (£8.99)
___ Teaching Someone to Drive (£8.99)
___ Travel Round the World (£8.99)
___ Understand Finance at Work (£8.99)
___ Use a Library (£7.99)

___ Use the Internet (£9.99)
___ Winning Consumer Competitions (£8.99)
___ Winning Presentations (£8.99)
___ Work from Home (£8.99)
___ Work in an Office (£7.99)
___ Work in Retail (£8.99)
___ Work with Dogs (£8.99)
___ Working Abroad (£14.99)
___ Working as a Holiday Rep (£9.99)
___ Working in Japan (£10.99)
___ Working in Photography (£8.99)
___ Working in the Gulf (£10.99)
___ Working in Hotels & Catering (£9.99)
___ Working on Contract Worldwide (£9.99)
___ Working on Cruise Ships (£9.99)
___ Write a Press Release (£9.99)
___ Write a Report (£8.99)
___ Write an Assignment (£8.99)
___ Write & Sell Computer Software (£9.99)
___ Write for Publication (£8.99)
___ Write for Television (£8.99)
___ Writing a CV that Works (£8.99)
___ Writing a Non Fiction Book (£9.99)
___ Writing an Essay (£8.99)
___ Writing & Publishing Poetry (£9.99)
___ Writing & Selling a Novel (£8.99)
___ Writing Business Letters (£8.99)
___ Writing Reviews (£9.99)
___ Writing Your Dissertation (£8.99)

To: Plymbridge Distributors Ltd, Plymbridge House, Estover Road, Plymouth PL6 7PZ. Customer Services Tel: (01752) 202301. Fax: (01752) 202331.

Please send me copies of the titles I have indicated. Please add postage & packing (UK £1, Europe including Eire, £2, World £3 airmail).

☐ I enclose cheque/PO payable to Plymbridge Distributors Ltd for £

☐ Please charge to my ☐ MasterCard, ☐ Visa, ☐ AMEX card.

Account No.

Card Expiry Date [ ] [19] ☎ **Credit Card orders may be faxed or phoned.**

Customer Name (CAPITALS) ....

Address ....

.... Postcode ....

Telephone............................... Signature ....

Every effort will be made to despatch your copy as soon as possible but to avoid possible disappointment please allow up to 21 days for despatch time (42 days if overseas). Prices and availability are subject to change without notice.

| Code BPA |

970858   £9.99   NIBS